What people are saying about

Survive

Jerry, I read through your book and was bowled over by its breadth and depth, and by the scholarship in it, and by the clarity and fluency in your writing. Excellent!
Rick Hanson Ph.D., *New York Times* bestselling author of *Buddha's Brain*, and UC Berkeley psychology professor, and senior fellow of the Greater Good Science Center

Survive is an excellent-written book that presents valuable information on several aspects of survival; physiological, philosophical, psychological and spiritual. It provides awareness-raising techniques and coping strategies. This is a book for everyone, young and old.
Roma Runeson-Broberg Ph.D., retired associate professor, Uppsala University in Sweden and licensed psychologist/ psychotherapist

Jerry Pannone helps us make sense of our world and ourselves in his life-affirming book that goes deep, fast. *Survive* resonates in a powerful way, asking us to consider the questions of life: Why do we do what we do? And why does that matter? The author takes us on his journey of self-discovery and, by the end of the book, we can't help but have a greater understanding of our own life journey.
John Sharify, multi Emmy Award winner and 2021 DuPont-Columbia University Award-winning broadcast journalist and filmmaker

Survive

Why We Do What We Do

Survive

Why We Do What We Do

Jerry Pannone

PSYCHE BOOKS

Winchester, UK
Washington, USA

JOHN HUNT PUBLISHING

First published by Psyche Books, 2022
Psyche Books is an imprint of John Hunt Publishing Ltd., No. 3 East St., Alresford,
Hampshire SO24 9EE, UK
office@jhpbooks.com
www.johnhuntpublishing.com
www.psyche-books.com

For distributor details and how to order please visit the 'Ordering' section on our website.

Text copyright: Jerry Pannone 2021
jerrypannone.com

ISBN: 978 1 80341 090 6
978 1 80341 091 3 (ebook)
Library of Congress Control Number: 2021949925

A CIP catalogue record for this book is available from the British Library.

Design: Stuart Davies

UK: Printed and bound by CPI Group (UK) Ltd, Croydon, CR0 4YY
Printed in North America by CPI GPS partners

We operate a distinctive and ethical publishing philosophy in
all areas of our business, from our global network of authors to
production and worldwide distribution.

Contents

To my dear wife
Elizabeth
Thank you, for everything

Preface

In some ways, the research for this book took my entire life. I say that because it is fundamentally based on lived experiences. By that I mean that theoretical knowledge can only truly be understood when it moves to the practical or, in our personal history, the lived. I could not have assimilated that understanding into my consciousness without those lived experiences, which in turn, gave me the confidence to write this book.

The writing of this small volume took about a year and I call it my COVID-19 project. Most of us have spent the better part of the last year at home. The lockdown of just about the whole planet was an unexpected event that took the majority of us by surprise.

The question became what to do with the time? Some had the luxury of working at home and, whether they liked the prospect of it or not, they were at least able to make a living. Many people were essential workers who had to go out because of the necessity of their services to the rest of society: food workers, health care workers, and numerous other service industry employees we all depend on for daily survival had to be the brave ones. And, of course, a great number of people lost their jobs and businesses due to the pandemic and consequently this has been an extremely rough period for them. But for people like me, retired and living on a pension, well, we just stayed at home and made the best of it. So I wrote a book.

I spent the majority of my life as a musician and music teacher, along with some teaching in the humanities. I've also always had a love of philosophy and psychology and felt these two disciplines, along with science, hold the cognitive keys to the bigger questions in life. Wondering about those bigger questions made me reflect on why I even began wondering. Oddly enough I traced it back to music.

I grew up in a chaotic household where petty disputes were the norm and, on many occasions, very intense. From the age of ten, I used music as an escape from the nightly conflicts. My drums offered an invitation to another world, one filled with peace and joy and occasionally even ecstasy. My practice sessions became, in fact, addictive.

My young mind hadn't yet begun considering the deeper questions of life—why things happen as they happen, why do we do what we do, and who is the I in the question, "Who am I?" It was only years later, when I joined the army in 1962 that I began meeting people who sparked these deeper questions in me through their own explorations of life and self. In the military, these sorts of thoughts and explorations crop up naturally perhaps because one's very existence feels very tenuous.

On the other hand, my own military experience was pretty cushy. I was in an army band stationed in Verona, Italy. This was before the Vietnam War and was, all in all, not a bad way to spend your time in the military. One day while browsing through books in the army base library, I ran across philosopher-psychologist Eric Fromm's insightful book *Man for Himself.* I confess that at first I barely understood a word, but with patience the words began making sense and I became introduced to a corner of the intellectual world I felt compelled to continue exploring. Over the next several years, I devoured all I could get my hands on and when I decided to finally go to college, I had a hard time deciding on a path of study between my equally divided loves of music, philosophy, and psychology. But with a wife and two children by that point, I decided in the end on the one I thought would just get me through quickly so I could start making a living. Music it was and with my degree I began a long career teaching music in the San Francisco Bay area, with the majority of those years spent at the Ruth Asawa School of the Arts High School in San Francisco.

After some years of teaching music behind me, I found myself wanting more intellectual stimulation and began returning to my earlier philosophical explorations and started a greater focus in my teaching on the humanities, in general, and philosophy, specifically. I developed and taught a critical thinking and ethics class, sponsored a philosophy club, and in collaboration with the San Francisco State University Philosophy Department, helped start National High School Ethics Bowl debate teams for two schools. Philosophy graduate students coached many of the high school teams. We competed annually for six years at the Northern California Regional competitions held at the University of California Santa Cruz Philosophy Department.

Those who do not teach high school may be surprised at how deeply high school students can and do think when given positive encouragement and opportunity. It gives me great hope for the future, in fact, and I've become an ardent proponent of including philosophy in public school curriculum.

Outside of knowing all the workings of the universe, and the Theory of Everything (TOE), I think we all just want to be happy, and having an understanding of our motivations and behavior can help us on that path.

I've been so inspired not only by my students but by the authors I have read and studied over many years. I feel immensely indebted to these great thinkers who have enriched my life. My sincerest hope is that this book provides the reader with some portion of what I've gleaned and that it will open the reader's world just that much more.

Acknowledgments

Just as one of the main themes of this book is interconnectedness, so too is the reality that we do very little that is not directly or indirectly dependent on the efforts and expertise of others. I'm deeply indebted to Rick Hanson, UC Berkeley psychology professor, and senior fellow of the Greater Good Science Center at Berkeley for his early reading of this book, his insightful suggestions, and his excellent endorsement. Also, to Roma Runeson-Broberg Ph.D. retired associate professor from Uppsala University for her very positive endorsement. Many thanks to Ruth Anne Phillips for her final edit. Her experience and expertise consistently showed me how I could improve this work and go beyond my original perceptions by making the necessary connections of thematic content within the work. More thanks than I can possibly express to Robert and Marsha Clark for their excellent early proofreading and insightful suggestions for additions and editing, without which this work would have suffered immeasurably. Thank you to Irina Melnik and Dan Matthies for providing me with places to work in two beautiful locations, which allowed me to focus on the writing of this work. Thank you to Theo Colbert, and Galina Ermolin, and the members of the Silicon Valley Humanist Book Club, that introduced me to many of the works and authors that I have quoted in this book. Thank you to Brock Honma for the cover format. Thank you to all my colleagues, dear friends, and family, for the many wonderful conversations and the influence that you've had on me over many years which have contributed significantly to the ideas that have found their way into this work. You are all my teachers.

Introduction

Remember those wildlife documentaries of salmon swimming upstream to spawn? The struggle was intense—climbing small waterfalls, forging through rapids that exhausted their strength, narrowly escaping bears who hoped to fatten themselves up for winter. The salmon had to reach their spawning grounds to lay their eggs, and even though each female salmon laid thousands of eggs, only a few lived to see adulthood. I can still feel myself identifying with these incredible fish, rooting for them, hoping they would not suffer the claws of the bear or lack the strength to overcome all the obstacles they faced on their arduous journey to spawn and then die. This drama of life to reproduce their line for their kind to survive is what all living organisms face, from the amoeba to the human being. The instinct for self-preservation is the single-most crucial drive that maintains our existence.

This drive for survival sends humans seemingly always hurtling forward. Unceasing new inventions and technologies spew forth at what feels like lightning speed, transforming our experience and understanding of our place in the world. Whole fields like evolutionary biology, quantum physics, and organic electronics join and change to produce ever rising new fields. And yet, despite all this seeming change and forward movement, the old adage "the more things change, the more they remain the same" holds. Despite all that happens around us, we are still inextricably stuck with the human condition. It is what it is and has been for millennia. This is the reason ancient writings from the Greek and Roman philosophers to the great books of the religions all still resonate with us today. It's why explorations of archaeological remains are so familiar to us. From Plato and Confucius to our present-day philosophers and great thinkers, we all ponder many of the same perennial issues.

All that comprises the essentials of human existence—birth, growth, emotionality, aspiration, conflict, mortality—pushed our forebears as much as they do us. These are the fundamentals of survival.

Although the concept of survival is evident in a biological sense, it expands far beyond simple physical survival for the human being. The questions of psychological, emotional, intellectual, and spiritual survival, as well as the overriding question of identity all play a role. Who is the "me" that is fighting to survive? That is the existential question we struggle consciously or unconsciously to address.

In the plant world, the struggle for survival is evident in a plant leaning toward the Sun to capture its rays for photosynthesis. The process is at once life-giving to the plant and a function of purpose. The Sun's rays result in the chemical transformation that allows the plant to thrive and to transform carbon dioxide into oxygen, which, in turn, permits all other oxygen-breathing beings to survive. On the one hand, this interconnectedness appears to be self-evident, yet there are still those who resist its truth.

When we try to pick anything out by itself, we find it hitched to everything else in the universe. ~ John Muir

The reality of this interconnectedness is gradually gaining acceptance as science begins to offer more proof of our interdependency with nature. Using the planet for our own ends with no regard for consequences is a practice many of our fellow planetary citizens find difficult to move beyond. We can recognize many reasons for this brazen indifference: poverty; regional wars over land issues, religion, or resources; and the global problem of societies still trying to play catch-up with the industrialized world. Some developing countries have expressed that they cannot afford the luxury of investing in renewable energy sources. Therefore, they must depend more heavily on fossil fuels, which negatively affects the global environment.

In the end, however, doesn't the awareness of the Earth's precarious position revolve around a fundamental and collective understanding of survival? The limited view of our connectedness to the whole is a function of our level of awareness. *The Cambridge English Dictionary* defines *awareness* as "knowledge that something exists or an understanding of a situation or subject at present based on information or experience." Since we are always limited by the lens of our own perception in terms of the information we take in or what we experience, it should not be surprising that we are inclined to view our own survival needs differently than those of others.

If we use a rubric like Abraham Maslow's Hierarchy of Needs, we can see some areas where there would be a consensus, at least concerning those fundamental needs. For the purpose of this book, I've used Maslow's Hierarchy of "expanded" needs as an outline. The original needs included: (1) Physiology (2) Safety (3) Love and Belonging (4) Esteem and (5) Self-actualization.[1] To those original needs, three more were later added by Maslow during the 1960s and '70s with some reordering. I've listed them here with abbreviated definitions:

(1) Physiology: water, food, air, shelter, sex
(2) Safety: protection, security, order, limits, stability, etc.
(3) Love and Belonging: family, affection, relationships, etc.
(4) Esteem: achievement, status, responsibility, etc.
(5) Knowledge and Understanding: comprehension, meaning, self-awareness
(6) Need for Aesthetics: beauty, balance, form, etc.
(7) Self-actualization: personal growth, self-fulfillment
(8) Transcendence: going beyond the self to Highest levels of human consciousness

Abraham Maslow's (expanded) Hierarchy of Human Needs

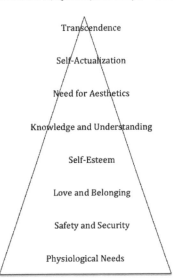

Maslow's Hierarchy of Expanded Needs

Maslow viewed these needs as "motivational needs." They are what motivate us to act—but act for what? Personal growth, advancement in society, and acceptance fundamentally point to the underlying need to survive. This is my interpretation of Maslow's Hierarchy, which I go into more deeply in Chapter 2. In the following chapters, we will explore how this drive for self-preservation or survival becomes the foundational motivator for action in every living organism. We will also see in the first chapter that this process is even true for those organisms without a brain or nervous system. When this process is recognized, we begin to ask the more profound questions that go to what we will do to survive at every level of Maslow's Hierarchy and beyond. If even just those higher needs are thwarted, or there is a danger to the defenses, which protect them, that condition would be considered a psychological threat, which Maslow believed to be a cause of the majority of the pathologies in the human experience. Here I'll just interject that Maslow's Hierarchy is merely one model for human development and although I chose it as an overall outline, other models will be referenced in the course of the book to supplement Maslow's theory.

The Roman writer Terence (195–159 BC) once said, "Nothing that is human is foreign to me." The breadth of thought and action inferred by that statement leaves nothing out of the realm of the human condition, nor what humans are capable of doing from the most banal and gruesome to the highest levels of saintly accomplishment and bliss. We are capable of it all and all of it in one form or another has to do with survival or, more importantly, what we believed we needed to do to survive.

No reasonable person would disagree with the first few levels of Maslow's Hierarchy (bottom-up). Physiological needs include food, water, air, and shelter existing in an overall state of homeostasis. Anything jeopardizing these basic necessities is viewed as an impediment to our basic survival. The concept of survival exists on all levels of Maslow's Hierarchy, not just the lower physiological needs. He states: "I should say simply that a healthy man is primarily motivated by his needs to develop and actualize his fullest potentialities and capacities."[2]

In this sense, there is a difference between surviving and just existing. In a very real way, merely existing infers stasis, yet nothing in life stays the same. Surviving means, to some degree at least, moving forward. The life-affirming aspects outstep the life-negating forces for the organism to prosper, even if that prospering is not always optimal, since some individuals will choose to live at very "simple" levels of acquiring the lower needs in order to pursue more satisfying intellectual or artistic higher needs they may consider more self-actualizing.

The challenges of life are seldom equal for all forms of living organisms. There are those born with a silver spoon and others with no spoon at all. This is true for all life forms within the same categories and species. Conditioning, adaptation, genetics, all have a part to play in the game. All things are in a state of change, and all actions are, to some degree, again either life-affirming or life-negating. Even mountains grow through geological movement and slowly die through the process of erosion.

In the cosmological realm, stars are born, grow, and die. In the world of living organisms, everything is either growing or dying. Furthermore, in some cases, those actions are happening at the same time in the same organism. Individual cells may die within an organ while, at the same time, that organ is growing. We may be physically declining but intellectually growing. The end of life, however, cuts off any growth altogether. Well, that is, if we exclude the organisms created by decaying entities or allusions to an afterlife. In a conversation with an atheist friend concerning the possibility of an afterlife, for example, I made the statement that "I could not conceive of not being." My friend's retort to me was, "death is the end of conceiving." I had to admit, true or not, it was a good point, especially since neither of us could prove differently.

Every language becomes bound by the discipline for which it is used. It is to a lesser or greater degree representational. Perhaps the fact that many of the humanities and the arts have "languages" that can be more malleable than that of science is because they are conveying realities that do not lend themselves to those restrictions necessary for the sciences. And these languages within the arts vary from discipline to discipline. Dance conveys a quality of experience that music cannot. Likewise, music has a quality that visual arts do not possess and vice versa. We must experience these arts individually to understand what they want to convey. Obviously, this is true of other endeavors.

For whatever reason, we may be personally attracted to some art forms more than to others. And in the world of academics, it is the same. A person gifted in mathematical abilities may not have a great facility with the written word and so on. But most would agree that our horizons are broadened and enriched by exposure to a variety of experiences. Howard Gardner's work on the theory of multiple intelligences goes a long way toward showing how we are all gifted in different ways.[3] That giftedness Gardner says is a form of intelligence, although they all wouldn't show up on an IQ test. He is up to about twelve forms of intelligence that he has identified, from mathematical to interpersonal intelligence. And for those folks who seem to never get lost or lose their car in a parking lot, he would say they have higher levels of visual-spatial intelligence than others.

The theory, on its face, makes sense for the survival of society. If all our talents focused on the linguistic facility, who would fix our houses, cars, or plumbing? Who would be the scientists who make the great discoveries that have propelled the advancements in our quality of life? Who would satisfy our aesthetic needs? A saying often attributed to Einstein stated, "Everybody is a genius. However, if we judge a fish by its ability to climb a tree, it will live its whole life, believing that it is stupid." Sadly, our schools fail in recognizing what has been evident for centuries. We are all different, and our talents are different, but people must be valued for their contributions to the needs of an extremely complex societal web. Schools today focus on a narrow set of talents, which, although valuable, leave behind a significant number of students. Moreover, like Einstein's fish trying to climb a tree, they will forever be misjudged and feel stupid.

As we move up the ladder of Maslow's Hierarchy, we also must adjust the language to meet the challenges of those needs and, at some point, admit that perhaps language itself is not adequate to convey the necessary meaning. For example, in trying to address spiritual experiences, language can only point the way. By its nature, a spiritual experience is an experiential reality, which language, even the most poetic, cannot convey. It must be experienced to understand it.

This book has three parts, and although there are many sub-headings under each part, they are all linked by the single concept of what survival means at every level of existence, and the evolutionary perspective that appears to emerge from our explorations of this single fundamental drive. In conjunction with understanding our need to survive, we confront the question, "Who am I?" This seemingly simple question becomes increasingly complex as we plumb the depths of self-awareness, and explore the question of what is the "self" that is becoming aware?

Chapter 1 focuses on our physiological survival needs and gives examples from the most basic life forms with neither a nervous system nor a brain, showing the amazing ingenuity they've developed to cope with their own survival needs, that in many ways seems strangely familiar to our own behaviors. We then draw parallels between the animal and human worlds where in the past we did not believe we had any commonality—areas like cooperation, altruism, reciprocity, and even morality. Finally, we discuss the main differences between "them" and "us."

In **Chapter 2** we focus on the psychological aspects of Maslow's Hierarchy and see where those needs arise. We look at concepts of our ego-self, what that means, and how our development is explained by researchers like Sigmund Freud, Carl Jung, Lawrence Kohlberg, and others. One of the major current dilemmas we investigate is the concept of "free will," which has philosophically been debated for centuries, but now has also entered the world of neuroscience. We investigate how our beliefs are formed and how those beliefs are conditioned by our experiences, which in turn direct us to different philosophical schools of thought. We end this part with a discussion of Eric Fromm's views on narcissism and what it means for the survival of the ego-self.

Chapter 3 introduces a metaphysical component. Here we investigate the "flow" state and mindfulness meditation. At the same time, we're still connected to Chapter 2 with some of the same psychological issues that now manage to carry into Maslow's higher order of needs like Self-actualization and Transcendence. We look at concepts of transcendence and transformation in reference to the ego-self, which hangs on, literally for dear life. But what does that mean to the goal of survival, especially when the ego-self is tethered to the question of "who am I"? This journey is an interesting ride, and one that I hope we can all enjoy.

Chapter 1

Physiological Aspects of Survival

In this first chapter, we focus on relationships that appear to exist commonly throughout life and the awareness of which, benefits all in our mutual need to survive. The relationships, including issues of identity, are from the simplest organisms to the most complex: amoebas to humans and all other life forms that exist in the biosphere. What we soon discover is that what appears to be purely a study of physiological needs (on Maslow's lower level), is inextricably related to psychological and sociological needs and, though complexity increases as we move up the evolutionary tree, those basics seem to be embedded from our very earliest existence as life forms. And although they may not be self-evident (because of evolutionary limitations) from the organism's level of awareness, they are the foundations of everything along the survival road that follows: speciation, identity, individuality, cooperation, organization, and the beginning development of social norms and morality. But most importantly, the ongoing driving force to survive by both the individual and the group by whatever means necessary.

Life Will Out

Mythologist Joseph Campbell (1904–1987) believed "Life Will Out" to be a sort of cosmic law, though which specific cosmic law he meant is unclear. But the idea that life will find a way to survive under the harshest of circumstances is a fact of life on our planet.[4] Campbell's work, particularly his book *The Hero's Journey,* inspired filmmaker George Lucas to create his *Star Wars* movies.

We're coming to understand that all life forms in this world are part of an extended family, meaning inextricably linked one to another. The process we're exploring here is not meant to enumerate every kind of life along the evolutionary tree, from bacteria to humans, but to look for the common denominators up and down that tree, with some concentration on what has traditionally been considered the "higher" forms of life, since they are our closest relatives.

Charles Darwin's theory of natural selection simply put is "an explanation for adaptation and speciation." In other words, those individuals most able to adapt to their environment survived and reproduced."[5] Although, his theory is often reduced to "survival of the fittest," it doesn't mean simply the physically strongest, although that is often the case. Rather it means adaptation to the environment by whatever means necessary and viewing behavior as an evolutionarily adaptive trait.

Survival can be defined as living or continuing longer than, or beyond the existence of, another person, thing, or event — an outliving.[6] The basics for any organism to survive and reproduce are water and nutrients, plus a source of energy and a bit of space helps.

Maslow's first two needs, Physiology and Safety, are inextricably linked since the physiological needs cannot exist for long without safety and security. And these most basic survival needs are dependent on the following reality of survival: To acknowledge a process of outliving other things, we must accept that other things must die — plants or animals; we can't get away from the fact that we and other creatures eat something else in order to live. Breatharians may be an exception to this rule. Most claim to live off sunlight or energy from the universe and an occasional sip of water or so, but thus far there have not been enough people in that category to make a statistical difference, nor enough legitimate studies to prove their claims.

The will or instinct to survive at the lowest levels needs exploring before we move toward any other elements having to do with Maslow's motivational needs. Many of us have had the experience of going to a nursery and buying a plant for our garden or house. There usually is a tag, often tied to the plant, that spells out the amount of sun the plant requires — full, partial, or shade — as well as the type of soil best suited. If we choose to ignore these suggestions, we generally find that the plant, if it doesn't die completely will, in general, not do very well. The biological necessities of survival depend on the needs of the organism and the environmental support available to that organism. Up and down the chain of life we see continuity and balance. What is true of the microcosm is true of the macrocosm. Since looking at the microcosm is a simpler task, especially in the world of single-cell organisms, we're going to start at that point.

Once upon a time many believed that the Earth was flat. It seemed to make sense and the belief was unchallenged until Pythagoras came along in the sixth century BC and questioned its validity. Theories come and go, of course, and science is charged with the job of searching for truth, especially in the physical universe. With the invention of the microscope, the secrets of the natural world revealed beyond simple observation with the naked eye were amazing. Now, with the development of ever more powerful instruments, we can become like flies on the wall observing single-cell organisms and their behavior. Our understanding of the skills needed to survive at all levels of life is constantly enhanced with the invention of new technologies.

One question we are asking that we had presumed to know just a few decades ago is can a single-cell organism with neither nervous system nor brain have some rudimentary responses to stimuli that could pass as feelings of some sort? Before the present day, the presumption was no, it could not. And a little further back in time, most people didn't even believe other mammals could feel pain.[7] But in the past few years, some astonishing discoveries concerning the behavior of even single-cell organisms have been reported, which may require us to redefine what it means to feel something. A new area of research that is emerging called "basal cognition" is investigating forms of intelligence that do not require neurons and synapses.[8] This is important because prior to this age of evolutionary biological discovery we believed that only organisms with an intact neurological system were capable of any level of decision-making capacity. Now we know this capacity reaches much lower down on the tree of life.

Conditioned Behavior, Habituation, and Decision-Making

The idea of learning and decision-making was usually reserved for higher orders of life. We are beginning to learn to be a bit humbler in our initial assessments of the capacity of simple life forms, and as the following pages elucidate, survival depends on the ability to learn and learning permeates every aspect of our existence, and that of all sentient organisms.

Although we know that even bacteria can learn by adaptation to circumstances, that type of learning usually occurs over generations and is a product of evolution. Conditioned behavior, on the other hand, is a process for learning that was assumed to be restricted to organisms that had at least an evolved nervous system. Nobel prize winner Ivan Pavlov first discovered this type of conditioning with dogs in the 1890s. Animals are hardwired to salivate prior to feeding but Pavlov discovered that dogs would begin to salivate before they were fed, just by hearing sounds that precede their feeding. This "associative learning" or what we also call a Pavlovian response was thought to only exist in animals with a brain or at least a nervous system, but one research team composed of Israeli and Spanish scientists found that this type of learning also exists in amoeba proteus microorganisms. The researchers placed the amoebas in an electric field with food only on the positive pole of the field. The amoeba's natural tendency was to move to the negative pole, but they bucked this tendency and went toward the food on the positive side. The researchers then removed the food and observed that the amoebas still moved to the positive side indicating memory for the food on that side. This is also called *associative memory*, perhaps indicating the first evolutionary example of knowing which side of the bread is buttered.[9]

The second example is reported in a 2016 article published in *Science Daily* explaining how a team of scientists succeeded in showing that a single-celled organism, the *Physarum polycphalum* slime mold, which existed some 500 million years before humans, is capable of a type of learning called *habituation*. This is the process by which an organism has a decrease in response to stimuli after repeated presentations of that stimulus into its environment. For example, one can get habituated to sounds that are initially disturbing or distracting but over time are ignored or minimized. The cell also demonstrated some astonishing abilities. It could solve a maze, avoid traps, and optimize its nutrition, though little was known about its actual ability to learn.

In the experiment, the researchers introduced different groups of this mold with distasteful substances they needed to go through in order to reach food. Two of the groups confronted a "bridge" impregnated with quinine or with caffeine, with the control group going over a non-impregnated bridge. The two groups faced with the impregnated bridges were, at first hesitant about crossing through the substances, but gradually realized that they were harmless and crossed over them at an increasingly rapid rate. Through this experience the cell learned habituation. But after a period of two days of crossing the bridge without the impregnated substances the mold went back to its distrustful behavior.[10] What the experiment proved, however, is that what is first disturbing can be gotten used to if there is something of greater value that may be obtained by adapting to the aversive experience.[11]

My personal experience with this behavior was with our dog having a daily barking contest with our neighbor's dog. In our desperation for some sonic peace, we tried to find a device that would deter both dogs' barking and decided to try an ultra-high frequency gadget that was touted on the Internet as effective for the barking problem. It worked by emitting a high frequency sound that was annoying to the dog and triggered by the sound of the dogs' barks. We bought it and placed it on our backyard fence. It immediately stopped both dogs from barking after the first bark of either dog. We and our neighbor enjoyed about six weeks of a bark-free zone. After that, the dogs became accustomed to the high frequency sound, and to our great disappointment, returned to their barking routine.

But back to our slime mold. In perhaps an even more impressive behavior, the slime mold demonstrated a capacity to *teach* other members of its group. By fusing with another slime mold for a couple of hours, it can pass on the information on how to cross an impregnated bridge. The recipient was then able to use the information and cross the bridge in less time than the original explorer.[12]

The third example of a single-cell organism exhibiting learning behavior is the *Stentor roeseli*. The organism is a tiny trumpet-shaped protist, a single-cell organism similar to algae and fungi, that can dodge, duck, or flee in response to an irritating stimulus, changing its behavior when one strategy fails. The study suggests that single cells, rather than being preprogrammed to react in a certain way, are capable of "changing their minds based on experience."[13] The fact that different *Stentor roeseli* cells would behave differently under the same circumstances suggests that the cells possess a sort of autonomy.[14] We may discover that although they look the same, each one is slightly different. Could it be that with different sets of experiences, the individual conditioning is the reason for the different reactions or is there something more going on?

Does all this mean we need to reexamine our definition of what creatures are sentient?

One definition of sentience is "feeling or sensation as distinguished from perception and thought." So perhaps we can assume, as a result of these experiments, that even a single-cell organism can feel at some rudimentary level. Also, instead of a simple aversion to negative stimuli, what causes the *Stentor roeseli* to appear that they are somehow capable of "changing their minds"?[15] Can it make some rudimentary decisions without a brain or nervous system and are those decisions in any real way volitional? Thus, one Stanford University observer was prompted to say, "It's fascinating that a single cell that is not a neuron has everything it needs to make a decision."[16] There may be a tendency to believe that all of these microscopic organisms follow the same pattern within a group. However, scientists have discovered that many of these groups contain "loners" that appear to march to the beat of their own drum. Does this indicate a level of individuality even at the single-cell level of life? And might these loners be the pathfinders of the microbial world?[17]

Are the three above behavioral responses exhibited by these organisms all just adaptive chemical reactions to stimuli, devoid of any other components, or do these experiments show that the smallest organisms are capable of learning and even possess the capacity for feeling and that both learning and feeling are inextricably connected to the organism's capacity for survival? Feeling pain, for example, is a universal avoidance mechanism that lets us know something is wrong. It's a necessary component of survival. In the amoeba it may simply be a stimulus response reflex action, but how that takes place with no nervous system is part of the mechanics of discovery yet to be understood.

Fear, too, may be a learned response, and even in the amoeba there appears to be something that looks like fear in its avoidance reaction to negative stimulation before harm actually takes place. Both fear and pain, though refined in higher animals and humans, appear to be present, at least to some degree, in these microscopic forms. The triggers that activate our instinctual sense of self-preservation and the fight or flight response are primarily fear and anxiety or stress, which are fundamental biological responses to survival threats.[18] At this stage, it's also necessary to separate feeling or sensation as distinguished from the cognitive capacity for perception and thought.

Cognition exists down through all the different life forms with each organism and part knowing its job and proper place. They are all gifted with individual competencies whether they are single cells or multicellular organs or tissues. They each embody the nuts and bolts of information to do what is needed to fulfill their function. They don't need to be conscious, at least not in any sense that we generally understand consciousness, but they do need to be structured in a way that enables them to use information to perform tasks starting with the main task of self-preservation, and that involves the ability to adapt to their local environment to advance their prospects.[19]

In an attempt to find early illustrations of the smallest organisms' actions toward self-preservation, I used the above-mentioned single-cell organisms as examples of what actions are possible without a brain or nervous system. We can put viruses aside, since the definitions for biological life still puts them in a gray area with no solid consensus at present as to whether they constitute a living organism.

Today, sciences like evolutionary biology, neurosciences, and evolutionary psychology force us to constantly reevaluate our assumptions about the limits of our understanding concerning motivation and the cause-and-effect responses of the smallest creatures in the biosphere. There is still much we simply do not understand concerning the life forces at work on the planet. But one thing appears to be clear and for that, a phrase from the movie *Jurassic Park* comes to mind: "Life will find a way."

Sentience

The entire definition of *sentience* is a "feeling or sensation as distinguished from perception and thought." In consideration of that definition, sentience seems to be creeping further and further down the biological tree of life to the point where we now even have organizations creating journals on the subject: *"Animal Sentience" ASent* publishes current empirical findings on what, when, and how nonhuman animals feel, along with the practical, methodological, legal, ethical, sociological, and philosophical implications of the findings.[20]

This concern for the welfare of sentient beings is by no means new. Buddhist monks often walk with their heads looking down in order not to consciously harm any sentient being. And the Jains, a minority religious group in India, which constitutes about 1% of the population, are, we might say, an extremist sect for not wanting to hurt any living thing, including microbes if they can help it. During monsoon season, for example, the Jains forgo travel to avoid splashing through water so that microbes living in the water will not be harmed. The Jains posited the existence of microbial life well before they appeared under Western microscopes.[21] The Jains are an extreme group, of course, but here in the practical world of the twenty-first century many people still believe that animals do not feel pain. Does that enable us, in some way, to hurt them? Do we intentionally disconnect their suffering to go trophy hunting? Does the economic advantage of factory farming color our attitudes about the way we treat animals?

From life at the microbial level to the galactic, death is the constant companion of life. Animals come to those of us in the United States in plastic wrap: steaks, pork chops, ground beef, chicken, and fish. True, some markets still have a few things that resemble the animal we are consuming—fish in particular—but much fewer than in our grandparents' day. When was the last time we saw a pig's head staring at us in a food superstore?

Over the years, we have sanitized death, particularly the dead things we eat. We specifically don't like looking at dead faces. Perhaps it is the evolutionary closeness of some animals. The closer they are to us, the less tolerance we have for looking into their cold dead eyes at the meat counter. Dissociation becomes more difficult. According to biomedical professor Michael Woodruff, of Quillen College of Medicine, "The 'face of the other' in an animal, increases the likelihood that we will have a special relationship to that animal, which gives it status in our moral community."[22] We give dogs that kind of face, for example, as evidenced by the names we give them and the high moral favor in which we hold them in our communities.[23]

Most of us today do not live close to the land. We live in suburbs or canyons of concrete and steel, only venturing out into the forests or countryside as temporary escapes to reconnect with the earth. That reconnection, however, seldom involves a hard look at the death that sits just below the surface all around us. The great majority of us don't hunt for our food. We may have a garden with some fruits and vegetables, but we don't get on a tractor and plow the land or go into the forest with a gun to hunt for our dinner, those who fish or hunt for sport notwithstanding.

The number of farmers in the world has been getting smaller for generations as corporate farming has gradually begun to replace the family farm. That means that fewer have knowledge about how our food is produced. Once when I was about ten years old, I visited my uncle's family on his small farm. It was probably only about 60 acres or so, but they had some sheep, goats, and chickens as well as a cornfield and small pasture that a meandering creek passed through. I had two cousins on the farm—Joe who was a year younger than me and Marietta, who was about five. On the day I visited, Joe and I played in a field, chasing a small herd of sheep and goats behind the large barn that stored hay and the old tractor that was used to plow the fields. I can still remember laughing at how the young lambs bounded about seemingly joyful in their freedom to just run. In the midst of our play, my Uncle Sam, Joe's dad, called him from behind the barn and asked him for help. After about five minutes I decided to go look for Joe and see what he was doing. When I rounded the side of the barn, I saw my cousin holding a bowl below the head of a lamb my uncle had just slaughtered. The lamb was hanging by its hind legs from a tree branch. My uncle had slit the animal's throat; Joe was matter-of-factly catching the blood dripping from the lamb's neck into the bowl. Shocked, I quickly went back around the barn and vomited.

Life had given me my first real experience of death. We had just been playing with those lambs. But real life on a farm, until that experience, had been hidden from me. How could we play with an animal and then in the next moment kill it? Was there some dissociative process the mind goes through to allow that to happen? This was also my first experience with the concept of relativism. Until that point, I could only understand my cousin's life as somehow an extension of my own. We were similar in age; we had gone to some of the same events, birthday parties, Christmas celebrations, weddings, and assorted other occasions. What I didn't know was that my cousin Joe actually lived on a farm with all that is involved with that life.

Farm living had nothing at all to do with my experiences. What was normal and acceptable for him was simply not normal nor acceptable for me. But, why not? After all, I ate meat. Where did I think it came from? It had never occurred to me that outliving something else might mean killing and eating that something else so that I could survive.

In the present age, our choices abound as to which philosophy we choose to consider when and if we tussle with our conscience over what we could or should eat. Social psychologists have discovered an interesting hypothesis for the meat eaters among us. They found that humans who eat meat don't attribute the characteristics of sentience to animals they eat to the degree that do vegetarians. This denial of sentience allows for a degree of cognitive dissonance to enter the picture, since if the animal is not sentient it does not suffer. Thus, we human carnivores can mentally disengage from the harsh images of industrial farms and slaughterhouses and eat our meals in comfortable oblivion. We can see, therefore, that if sentience is denied, moral concerns can conveniently be put aside.[24]

I must admit to experiencing this chain of thinking myself. Thinking about sentience, when it comes to a food source that I've grown up with all my life is bothersome. In fact, in my teenage years, I along with my uncles and cousins went hunting together, answering to some primal urge of manhood. I gave it up after killing too many rabbits and pheasants for my own liking and asking myself what the hell I was doing in the woods with a 12-gauge shotgun (similar to a handheld canon), hunting down some innocent bunny? And the unpleasant thoughts of my cousin Joe and the slaughtering of the lamb began coming back to me. Of course, those thoughts didn't convince me to stop eating things that other people killed. Other people were doing those things, not me. Perhaps Woodruff is right: Cognitive dissonance gives us permission to justify our actions without any real self-reflection on what we're doing. It gives us plenty of space for self-justification.

Philosophers and scientist alike fall on either side of the divide regarding which animals are sentient. Ultimately, that belief is the arbiter of whether we would like to have a certain food on our dinner plate. In my own experience of flirting with vegetarianism, I've wondered just how long it will take to stare into the eyes of a cow before I see my own reflection?

Survival of the Fittest

Fear of us being a food source for a predator or the need to find a food source ourselves and all that it entails consumed the life of our predecessors from the microbial world up through our hunter-gatherer ancestors. And, given some of the unfortunate circumstances our fellow humans find themselves in today, we might extend that condition to the present.

There's a misconception that survival of the fittest means survival of the most aggressive. A better definition is "whatever leads to reproductive success," what Darwin called "natural selection," or the preservation of favored races in the struggle for life who are better adapted for the immediate local environment.[25]

It's not the strongest of the species that survives, nor the most intelligent. It is the one that is most adaptable to change.
~ Charles Darwin

Perhaps one aspect of Darwin's genius was his ability to observe nature and discern those qualities that most aid survival and not be distracted by what was simply obvious to the eye. It's easy, for example, to pick out the strongest in a species or with a bit more observation, which might be the most intelligent, but survivability is more complex. It knows intuitively which way the political winds in our group are blowing. Many functionary positions in the world of humans will allow us to live a long life. On the other hand, most of our names will probably not be written in any history books. Putting moral turpitude aside, there are some folks or organisms, for that matter, who can thrive in just about any conditions. They simply adapt to whoever or whatever the power structure is and don't rock the boat. They are the survivors often because they have figured out how to play the safety and security game of not making waves. It may also be why the movement of the common denominator of human morality and societal norms appears to move too slow or too fast, according to each individual's moral barometer.

Benefits of Not Being a Nice Guy

Superficial observations deceive us. The biggest, the strongest, the bully in the pack, all appear to have the advantage in nature, up through humans, yet the bully's victories tend to be short-lived. However, for someone on the receiving end of bullying, "short-lived" may seem like a very long time, and to be fair to the strong man mystique, bullying is still a successful evolutionary strategy for some and has great appeal in many species for survivability.

In the process of studying one chimpanzee pack, the primatologist Jane Goodall discovered that "Frodo," the alpha male of the group, threw rocks at the other chimps as a way of intimidating them and would often bite the other males in the group to keep them in line. Bullying one's way to the top is common in many animal groups, particularly with primates, and that behavior also goes hand in hand with the concept of pecking orders, which serves to maintain status within a group. Sadly, then, one individual is always on the bottom. It's also not as if Frodo were trying to benefit the group by his behavior. He's just doing what he needed to do to get what he wanted, which is usually females in the group.

We will not let Frodo off the hook so easily though. It turned out that bullies have a hard time maintaining any popularity. Frodo's behavior eventually caught up with him. After ruling for five years, he became weaker and the other males attacked him and threw him out of the pack. He lived alone for a time and when he returned, he was demoted to a very low rank in the group. He eventually died, possibly from a violent attack. Frodo's brother, Freud, on the other hand, was also the leader of the group before Frodo. He was far more conciliatory to the others in the group and enjoyed popularity by grooming the other chimps. He also left his leadership role peacefully and maintained a higher position when he left his alpha male position. Perhaps, at least in this case, there is an argument that leaders who are loved have a better chance at long-term survival than those who are feared.[26]

Fear and Stress

Fear is the handmaid of the survival instinct. It starts with a chain reaction in the brain triggered by a stressful stimulus, causing the release of chemicals (cortisol and adrenaline). The heart rate and breathing increase, which energizes the muscles. The stimulus could be anything that causes an excitable response: seeing a snake, walking alone at night, seeing a group of men approaching, or going outside for the first time during a pandemic—anything that diminishes our sense of security, both real and imagined. This includes things that are so subtle they are below our sense of conscious awareness. Our minds create numerous scenarios that activate a fear response, and the brain reaction undergoes a particular order in its response as follows:

- Thalamus—decides where to send incoming sensory data (from eyes, ears, mouth, skin)
- Sensory cortex—interprets sensory data
- Hippocampus—stores and retrieves conscious memories; processes sets of stimuli to establish context
- Amygdala—decodes emotions; determines possible threat; stores fear memories
- Hypothalamus—activates the "fight or flight" response

If we are one of the unfortunate individuals in the human or animal world who finds that they're on the low end of the societal totem pole, environmental stress becomes a problem. The effects of stress on animals are very similar to that of humans. One is the aforementioned release of adrenaline and cortisol hormones as part of the fight or flight response due to environmental pressure, another is the temporary suppression of the immune system. Some stress is necessary and it can even help some people perform beyond their expectations, as chronicled by the reports of those showing incredible strength in fighting off animals or lifting cars to save trapped individuals.[27] But a system constantly under stress is destructive. In general, calm is better for health, with just enough stress in the mix to keep life from becoming too boring.

That chemicals are released in our brains that affect our behavior is nothing new, but the contemporary study of both the origins and effects of the release of those chemicals is of primary importance when we begin to study why we do what we do. For an in-depth study of this area please see Robert Sapolsky's *Behave: The Biology of Humans at Our best and Worst*.[28] Not only does Sapolsky, a Stanford biology and neurology professor, explore the latest scientific discoveries in biology but he does so in the fields of psychology and sociology as well. He brings his exceptional analytic abilities to bear on human behavior, recognizing it as an extremely complex area with interactions among various disciplines.

Greed as a Biological Drive

Greed is one drive getting a larger piece of the pie and more of the necessary resources than other motivators. Greed is about relative wealth—how we stack up against our neighbors and the insatiable need for more. Is there a biological advantage for greed when it comes to self-preservation? It seems at some level there is, but in the end, greed is similar to bullying. It may get us what we want in the short run but tends to be detrimental for society-building and long-term cohesion. But first, let's look at the short run.

At this level, it makes biological sense to have at least a superficial view of evolution being a zero-sum game where there is a single survivor or very limited number of species the environment will support.

Many animals, especially primates and particularly humans,

have evolved social structures that allow for both cooperation and competition. When it comes to greed, competition takes the upper hand and fear of scarcity prompts action. The limbic system moves us to hoard more resources than we need. We especially experienced this at the beginning of the COVID-19 pandemic. Fear drove our primitive, visceral, gut reaction that says better safe than sorry, coupled with the herd instinct that makes us do what everyone else is doing. Buy more toilet paper as well as more food than we can eat in a month. If everyone else is panic buying, why shouldn't we do the same? After all, we don't know when this might be over and what if the markets run out? We need to survive until this is over (with an emphasis on "we" in the smallest sense).[29]

Cooperation in Groups for Survival

We often only think about humans cooperating to survive the challenges that confront us. But the more we learn about the natural world, the more we see cooperation in all species as being ubiquitous rather than the rare exceptions. And unless we become too animal-centric in this regard, it appears that even plants can communicate, not only within their own families but also with other organisms.

Prof. Monica Gagliano, researcher and associate professor in evolutionary ecology at the Biological Intelligence (BI) Lab at Southern Cross University in Lismore, Australia, and her group have been exploring the interesting world of plant communication through sound waves. She writes that plants produce sound waves that vibrate in the lower end of the audio range, and they also produce ultrasonic sounds. Her team captures the signals emitted by the plants under different environmental conditions. They then explore the ecological significance of how these sounds are used to communicate among plants and other organisms.[30]

As we begin to explore the natural world more deeply, the

phrase "the interconnectedness of all living things" is not just a bit of woo-woo New Age gibberish, but a reality we are only now beginning to understand. As one example, chimpanzees and bonobos practice cooperative actions that have more sophisticated attributes than most other animal species. This doesn't mean that other species using similar practices do not exist, but chimps and bonobos have been studied extensively. The cooperative traits include partnering, having long-lasting relationships with groupmates based on "friendship," competition, and dominance. Partners must show a sense of loyalty, reliability, and reciprocity as well. They may also cooperate with a partner to fight for dominance with a rival. But between the two species—chimps and bonobos—bonobos are far friendlier and sustain that friendliness through adulthood. Chimpanzees, on the other hand, are more selfish. Where reproduction is concerned, the result is that the friendliest male bonobo is more successful than an unfriendly alpha male chimpanzee.[31] Cooperation among humans goes far beyond what chimpanzees or other animals are capable of doing. In comparison studies with three-year-old human children and chimps, the toddlers showed a much greater willingness to cooperate with each other to complete a task than did the chimps. This ultra-sociality compared to the chimps was a prime indicator of the advancement of humans, which the researchers believed had gone back to the difference in food gathering. Humans had developed the capacity to hunt large game, which required more cooperation and was perhaps due to the environment; this, the chimps had not been able to do, since their environment did not require them to develop that skill.[32]

Cooperation is a trait that any society needs to cultivate in order to function. In the hunter-gatherer societies, a hunting party needs cooperation to secure game, with a group having the best chance of a successful hunt. The concepts of cooperation and reciprocity are built into the endeavor for the survival of the group. The loner may get lucky and kill an antelope, but if he does not share it, he will soon find himself on the outside of the tribe with no support system. Although we're not sure if cooperation is an epigenetic trait that is heritable, meaning it can be passed down through generations, we do know that without it, survival is impossible.

Interspecies cooperation

Videos of dolphins show them herding fish to feed and fighting off a shark as a pod. In the world of mammals, this cooperation is not all that unusual. And this extends to a number of other species types. For example, fish, it seems, are in on the game of cooperation, even where interspecies collaboration is concerned. Cooperation for survival—maybe it's a good idea.

Redouan Bshary, who studies coral reef fishes' social behavior, observed groupers and moray eels in the Red Sea. Since groupers and morays are two of the region's top predators and are in competition for food, they would be expected to avoid each other, but Bshary saw them join together to hunt. Bshary first saw the grouper signal the eel with its head, the two then swam next to each other, while the eel dipped its head into crevices, scaring out fish and then getting a chance to feed on them next to the grouper. Bshary was amazed by this unforeseen cooperation, and would have gasped if he hadn't had a snorkel in his mouth.

This underwater observation was the first in a series of surprising discoveries that Bshary has made about fishes' social behavior. They can signal to each other and cooperate across species, but they can also cheat, deceive, console, or punish one another—even show concern about their reputations. "I have always had a lot of respect for fish," says Bshary. "But one after the other, these behaviors took me by surprise."

Bshary also conducted experiments measuring fish

intelligence, finding that the same species may exhibit different levels of knowledge, depending on their environment, which reinforced the idea that animals had to be observed in their natural habitat to gain any objective information and that even within the same species, changing habitats makes a difference.

This work has also substantially destroyed the proposition that fish are fundamentally dumb creatures only capable of the simplest behaviors. The work also challenged behavioral ecologists in the field of primatology since they have long claimed that animals such as monkeys and apes are the only ones to exhibit human-like behaviors like cooperation.

"Redouan has thrown down the gauntlet to us primatologists," says Carel van Schaik, an expert at the University of Zurich in Switzerland in orangutan culture. "He has made us realize that some of the explanations of primate intelligence that we have cherished don't hold water anymore."[33]

Reciprocity and Altruism

Reciprocity in evolutionary biology refers to mechanisms whereby the probability of future mutual interactions may favor the evolution of cooperative or altruistic behavior.[34] Chimpanzees regularly share food, particularly with kin, with the expectation that the favor will be returned. Reciprocity in the human world is a cornerstone of societal interaction. "I'll scratch your back if you scratch mine" is built into our understanding and acceptance of interpersonal relationships, starting with kin association, extending to friendships, tribe, etc.

Until fairly recently, altruism — that ability to act unselfishly for others — was considered a uniquely human quality. When animals cooperate, it's generally to help their relatives in order to have a better chance of passing down shared genes or, in the case of non-relatives, the possibility of having favors returned in the future. In the case of inter-species altruism, research done by Felix Warneken and colleagues at the Max Planck Institute for

Evolutionary Anthropology in Leipzig, Germany, found that in one experiment twelve out of eighteen semi-wild chimpanzees made the decision to go out of their way to help an unfamiliar human get a stick he was struggling to reach.[35]

Kin Selection

Kin selection is the evolutionary strategy that favors the reproductive success of an organism's relatives. We're selecting our kin for special treatment because our genes benefit, even if it means it's at a cost to our survival and reproduction.

In the animal and human worlds, self-sacrifice for our dear ones is nothing new, especially if it means our kind will go on. The closer the kinship, the more willing we are to make sacrifices. Just as greed and the hoarding instinct are directed toward personal survival, by extension, so is kin selection. Identification, by extension, becomes meaningful when that extension enhances our genes. Self-sacrifice for the overall good is a secondary gain from this initial capacity for a willingness to sacrifice for kin. In the human world numerous propaganda devices have been utilized to convince group members to sacrifice for the good of the group, a cause, or a glorious leader.

What's the Difference between Them and Us?

In one article Robert Sapolsky writes that chimps have complex social lives. They play power politics—will not only betray one another but also murder one another. They make tools and can teach the use of tools across generations. They can perform logic operations with symbols and have a relative sense of numbers. All these behaviors, though, don't come close to the complexities and layers of those of humans. Chimps, for example, do not have an aesthetic sense nor do they exhibit any spiritual sensitivity nor anything approaching the human capacity for irony or poignancy. So, what is the difference between them and us? Sapolsky attributes the difference to the number of neurons we have. Slug or human, all living organisms have a first cell that is committed to generating neurons. Each cell division gives rise to the possibility of higher forms of life. Go high enough with the number of cell divisions and you have a human brain. Miss a couple of those cell divisions and you have a chimp.[36]

According to Sapolsky it comes down to 2 percent. We have 2 percent more cells than the chimp.[37]

But before we infer that bigger is always better, we need to remember that Neanderthals had bigger brains than *sapiens*, but they did not survive. The key may be where in the brain is more. The size of the prefrontal cortex, the controller of executive functions in the brain, is much larger in humans compared to chimps. The executive functions control reflexive behaviors, planning and long-term goals, decision-making, problem-solving, and self-control. They're the higher-level cognitive processes that people tend to display with greater ability than do other animals. One could argue that these functions is what helps make human cognition unique.

It's also true that the prefrontal cortex is the last part of the brain to develop. It's not fully developed in humans until the mid-twenties for women and even later for men, generally not until the late twenties, and some researchers say age thirty. No wonder violent crime and high-risk behavior begin to diminish for people in their thirties and later. One of the upsides of this knowledge is that parenting skills are now being developed that take advantage of this information and recognize that age-appropriate behaviors often call for different parenting approaches that take this new information into account.[38]

Brain Development

In the developing brain, there are more than enough cells to fill the need. Many of those unneeded cells will simply die off. Does that disprove the survival hypothesis or simply encode the need for cell destruction? Is it a very rudimentary form of self-sacrifice for the greater good of the organism? And as questioned above, are single cells conscious at any level? Despite the tendency to look for a simple definition of consciousness, the work done today by science, especially in biology and neuroscience, shows that any final definition is still a moving target.[39]

Gender Advantage for Survival

Female mammals generally live longer than males. When it comes to humans, women also live longer than men, even during severe famines and epidemics. Hands down women have the advantage. Biologists are still busy looking into this, but across the world, it's simply a fact: women live longer.[40] As the gender equality movement erodes the male dominance paradigm in society, perhaps the age-old practice of men marrying younger women needs some reconsideration.

Numerous studies are showing differences between men's and women's brains, from size to rate of development and neural connectivity. The future may see sex-specific treatments for a host of conditions, including depression, addiction, schizophrenia, and post-traumatic stress disorder (PTSD).[41] As was said above, men's brains tend to mature later, particularly the prefrontal cortex, which modulates the more instinctual drives of our amygdala, and that gives our criminal justice system a headache. For generations, we have put the age of adulthood at eighteen, but all the research shows that a man's brain does not fully mature until typically his late twenties. Is it then fair to judge the action of a male eighteen-year-old who commits a crime in the same category as a thirty-five-year-old man who commits the same crime? Society in general is slow to catch up to the findings of science. Tradition, religion, societal norms, and of course, a firm belief in personal accountability and free will have a lot to do with our legal process. But how much of that decision-making process for an eighteen-year-old is "free" if his brain is not fully developed?

Is Self-Awareness Unique to Humans?

The mirror self-recognition test (MSR) is revered as a means of testing self-awareness. A scientist places a colored, odorless mark on an animal where the animal can't see it, usually the head or shoulder. If the animal looks in the mirror and spontaneously rubs the mark, it passes the exam. Successful species are said to understand the concept of "self" versus "other."

Strange as it might seem, not all animals can immediately recognize themselves in a mirror. Great apes, dolphins, Asian elephants, and Eurasian magpies can do this—as can human kids around age two. Now some scientists are welcoming another creature to this exclusive club: carefully trained rhesus monkeys. The findings suggest that with time and teaching, other animals can learn how mirrors work, and thus learn to recognize themselves—a key test of cognition. "It's a really interesting paper because it shows not only what the monkeys can't do, but what it takes for them to succeed," says Diana Reiss, a cognitive psychologist at Hunter College in New York City, who has given the test to dolphins and Asian elephants in other experiments.[42] Since the mirror test is the only one being used thus far, scientists are being challenged to discover other tests that may show that other animals may have a sense of themselves.

Competition

We all have our little fiefdoms, professional or otherwise. We tend to protect them with psychological, if not physical drawbridges, delineating the me-and-thee and the us-and-them. Although "the times they are a-changing," we still manage to claim territory in which to plant our egos to protect the all-important "me."

In a rain forest, there is greed for light. Trees die and fall and leave openings for the sun's light to penetrate the canopy so that other trees and foliage may race to take their spots. The race for sunlight creates winners and losers. The winners live to fill that hole in the canopy and the losers die due to lack of sunlight. The greed for sunlight means life. It appears similar to a single sperm (with rare exceptions) racing millions of other sperm cells to fertilize an egg, but for various reasons, one being that we now know that female biology mitigates against some sperm cells (maybe not handsome or smart enough), so those cells are eliminated at the beginning.[43]

For many decades, however, we believed this race was just another example of the survival of the fittest and the strongest winning the race. We could even look at it as an example of nature being fair. Now, if all things were equal, it would seem to be fair, but in truth, nothing in nature is fair or equal. Some things are bigger and stronger, even within the same species. Some living things are smarter or more beautiful or more adaptable to certain environments, and the things that do not measure up usually just die off. Fairness is a human moral construct that nature does not recognize. Nature does not concern itself with fairness or equality.

Some people are born with genetic proclivities for certain diseases that they will suffer and perhaps succumb to in their lifetime. Tay-Sachs disease is visited primarily upon central and eastern European Jews, sickle cell anemia on African Americans. Carry the wrong gene and we are susceptible to breast cancer. Cardiovascular disease and diabetes, although often due to diet, still can affect some ethnicities more than others. And now we are even finding that PTSD may have an epigenetic component that crosses generations and may very well affect the descendants of African American slaves as well as the children of holocaust victims. This may help give some credence to the justification for the concept of reparations for African Americans under consideration by some American politicians.

Overall, equality in nature can often appear to be a cruel joke.

Body type is difficult to get around when it comes to athletics, for example. How many short people have played in the NBA or small-boned skinny folks in the NFL? Attitude and desire mean a great deal, but without nature giving a helping hand, greatness is seldom achievable.

On the upside, some are born with the best genes possible for certain activities—again, sports being the most obvious. Michael Phelps is the most decorated Olympian athlete of all time, winning a total of twenty-eight medals. He was born with the perfect body for an Olympic swimmer. Swimmers tend to have longer torsos and shorter legs than the average person. Standing at 6 feet 4 inches, Phelps has the torso of a man who's 6 feet 8 inches tall and the legs of a man 8 inches shorter. This disproportionately large chest enables Phelps to power himself through the water. It also means his legs produce less drag (or water resistance) with each stroke. His wingspan (distance from fingertip to fingertip when arms are outstretched) is 3 inches longer than his height (6 feet 7 inches versus 6 feet 4 inches). The average person's wingspan is about the same as their height. Like many swimmers, Phelps has hyper-extended joints—but his double-jointed ankles bend 15 percent more than his rivals. Paired with his size-14 feet, his legs act like flippers, thrusting him through the water.[44] All of this along with other physical advantages, coupled with an indomitable drive to succeed, gives Phelps a step up on the competition.

If body type is an advantage in the physical world, what about brainpower in the mental world? We still aren't sure what makes a genius, but we do know it has something to do with the structure of the brain. The thalamus is different in the brain of a genius. The dopamine receptors in our thalamus determine, essentially, what gets through. Our brains process thoughts faster than we can sort through them. The thalamus and the dopamine receptors are fundamentally the places that these entire thoughts bottleneck. Thoughts that serve in some way are allowed to proceed, whereas others are stifled and, most of the time, never reach conscious thought.

In a genius brain there tend to be fewer of these dopamine receptors. Thus, the neck of the bottle tends to be wider, letting more thoughts come through. Consider the potential of creativity and problem-solving a person could have if more thoughts and solutions were allowed to emerge. Then there is just the amount of gray matter that refers to the darker tissue of the brain and spinal cord. In the brains of people who had over 130 IQ scores, there is simply a greater volume of gray matter. Larger amounts of gray matter mean that communication occurs more quickly. Pictures of Albert Einstein's brain, for example, reveal not only a thicker and greater amount of gray matter but more intricate folds throughout the gray matter, which also may be a factor in the brain of a genius.[45]

The nature/nurture argument goes on and we can be sure that doing our very best at whatever we put our hand to makes a great difference to the outcome. But countless musicians have practiced thousands of hours with excellent instruction and have not become other Mozarts. Like Michael Phelps, there was just something a little different. It could be the gift of perfect pitch also called absolute pitch, for example—that ability to simply hear a particular note and know automatically what the pitch is that is being played or sung. Although this talent or form of intelligence as Howard Gardner might put it, is relatively rare—about 1 in 10,000 people may have it—among musicians it is higher at approximately 4% of that population, especially if their training started before the age of six. Early music instruction does help to bring out what appears to be this genetic proclivity as well.[46] My own experience as a music teacher in an arts high school bore this out, since occasionally one of my music students had that ability. Research shows that it also appears to run in families. Two sisters in my school orchestra had this ability, and I later found out that their father also had it. All that said, like Michael Phelps's big feet and long arms, perfect pitch is a definite advantage if we are a musician.

Does all this have something to do with an evolutionary pecking order of our places in our respective tribal groups, whether in our professions or other societal constructs? Maybe. But as Robert Sapolsky said at the end of his book *Behave*, "it's complicated." Einstein was at the top of the heap when it came to physics, but his ranking as a father and husband leaves much to be desired. Beethoven's musical genius was accompanied by a deeply tortured private life, hardly to be envied by anyone. We are, in fact, much more than those professions in which we engage. We are whole multifaceted human beings with the pluses and minuses that distinguish us from every other person on the planet. And although our names may not grace the pages of a history book, they are written deeply in the annals of time.

Equality?

In constructing the American Constitution, Thomas Jefferson penned the statement: "We hold these Truths to be self-evident, that all men are created equal, that they are endowed by their Creator with certain unalienable Rights, that among these are Life, Liberty, and the Pursuit of Happiness."

Yes, he wrote, "All men are created equal," and yet Jefferson himself, along with many of the other founders, were slave owners who completely denied equality to Black people in America. In a slap at the hypocrisy of this fact, abolitionist Thomas Day wrote: "If there be an object truly ridiculous in nature, it is an American patriot, signing resolutions of independency with the one hand, and with the other brandishing a whip over his affrighted slaves."[47] But we know that a compromise solution had to be reached for the Southern states to go along with independence from Great Britain. That compromise was the three-fifths solution, in which slaves were not counted as whole human beings. This would allow Southern states to have more representation without having slaves counted under the "class of men" who were created equal, endowed by their creator with certain unalienable rights, "that among these are life, liberty and the pursuit of happiness." So, not "all men," but a class of men who were created equal.

Today we're tearing down statues of those whose moral behavior does not comport with current ethical values, in many cases with complete justification, particularly in the case of Confederate generals. The temptation to judge the past and those that lived in it by the ethical values of the present is sometimes overwhelming. We forget about the conventional wisdom of the period and paint historical figures with a broad brush and often excuse or self-justify our own tendency to overlook those inequities of society that we tolerate in the present to the detriment of our fellow citizens, or in a deeper understanding, of our fellow sentient beings. How then, will the future judge us regarding our own dance with hypocrisy, and do we think it helps us survive?

While we're on the subject, what is equal about all men or women? If one believes in spiritual things, perhaps souls are equal, but at least thus far that proposition is beyond our ability to prove in any scientific way. So, no, in the observable world "All men are created equal" is not true either. It may be an aspirational goal and an incredibly inspiring one that has been copied around the world. The belief in it has also made great strides in attempting to level the playing field of opportunity, and although we in America have not reached that goal, it gives us something to strive for even though it may, in any true sense, be unattainable. However, in a democracy, it's important to give equal opportunity to all citizens. How far a government and its people are willing to go to make that happen is the measure of the compassion and sense of justice of that democratic society. And our willingness to support the aspirations and dreams of others is always conditioned by our desires for advantage and access. Compare this with some socialist and certain communist states where the object is the advancement of the collective and the worth of the individual is always subservient to that of the collective. But let's not go overboard here. In every society, human nature is hard at work for an advantage over others. That said, in the old Soviet Union, for example, talent scouts would go out and look for young children who were particularly gifted in sports and other disciplines. Those who were especially talented were given all of the attention and expert training available that they individually could never possibly afford. There was a price to pay, of course. It often meant being sent to special schools with long absences from their parents and often missing out on any other activities that would enhance their overall development. But one might also say this of children in democracies where parents and children have to make similar sacrifices for the children to reach the highest levels of competition. They also must find the means to pay for it on their own. Honor and glory always exact a steep price.

The expectation of freedom to do what we want and become whatever we want is ingrained in the American ethos. It may be, in many regards, an illusion, but the optimism can be contagious, and it has always been one of the most compelling draws for immigrants to come to America from around the world. In some ways their success became a self-fulfilling prophecy. We attracted the best and the brightest (at least we did up until the present) and the opportunities afforded them bore fruit in the form of all kinds of inventions, increased knowledge and the overall advancement of American society, added to that was the monetary gain for those who contributed. It was an overall win-win situation.

Most kids while growing up, perhaps particularly in America, are asked the question, what would you like to be when you grow up? It may be just a fuzzy philosophical question to the child whose imagination lives in the world of childhood make-believe, but still, the possibility of choice in what the future may offer is an intoxicating dream. And there is no doubt that often the dream creates a reality that, without the expectation, the effort needed to realize the dream could not be accomplished: that ability to motivate and be motivated may be just as an important an outlier for determining success as anything else.

Stanford professor of psychology Carol Dweck has done a great deal of work on the psychology of motivation. She found there to be a vast difference between telling children who accomplish a difficult task, "You must be smart" versus "You must have worked hard." Praising children for working hard gives them the satisfaction of valuing accomplishment for its own sake and enjoying the process more than working just for getting the grade. Tell a kid they're smart and the opposite occurs. They end up believing that they shouldn't have to work very hard to accomplish anything. Having had the privilege of teaching many gifted music students, it quickly became obvious to me that terms like *talented* and *smart* are relative all up and down the scale of accomplishment. But there is no substitute for smart (talented) and hard work. It's important to recognize that all people possess some degree of both in many different fields of endeavor. What becomes the winning combination is a question for history books and paychecks or, for us lesser mortals, just family stories around the dining room table.

Charles Darwin posited that our emotions had a survival purpose when he proposed that emotions evolved because they were adaptive and allowed humans and animals to reproduce. Feelings of love and affection lead people to seek mates and reproduce. Feelings of fear compel people to either fight or flee the source of danger.[48] We will spend more time looking at emotions in Part 3, but we can't deny that drive and imagination owe a lot to our emotional attachment to goals.

Chapter 1

Morality and Biology

We are tempted to form moral arguments for or against propositions from only philosophical standpoints, but we're beginning to realize that even human morality has much of its foundation in neurobiological processes predating our entrance on the world stage.

Nearly 150 years ago, Charles Darwin proposed that morality was a by-product of evolution, a human trait that arose as natural selection shaped humans into a highly social species— and the capacity for morality, he argued, lay in small, subtle differences between us and our closest animal relatives.[49] In *The Descent of Man*, Darwin wrote, "The difference in mind between man and the higher animals, great as it is, certainly is one of degree and not of kind."[50]

According to biologist and primatologist Frans de Waal, "We tend to think of empathy as a uniquely human trait. But it's something apes and other animals demonstrate as well." Our evolutionary history suggests a deep-rooted propensity for feeling the emotions of others.[51] Without empathy, how can the tribe or for that matter, the human race survive? The subject of ethics, long thought to be the sole domain of moral philosophy, is beginning to be challenged by the natural sciences with their observations and experiments. What are the effects of brain chemistry and evolutionary adaptation on our behavior? Are ethical principles discerned by cognitive argumentation as the metric by which we discover the truth? And what about the concept of truth itself? What is objective truth and, if there is such a thing, can we know what it is? Reason itself is now believed to have evolved as an adaptive device for survival in groups, rather than the individual's search for any objective truth in a given circumstance. Some posit that moral decision-making is "an intuitive or emotional process," and that what we call "reason" is simply justification for actions that happen after this decision-making process has taken place. Reason, in this model, is not a "higher order" process and the concept of free will is challenged. This throws out the importance of understanding intentions before judging responsibility for action, which would ultimately have an enormous impact on Western ethical traditions.[52]

So, when doing the right thing intersects with one's survival, the circumstances often dictate the hierarchy of moral values. In the world of chimpanzees, we can both praise and pity the poor chimp that would put moral conviction above group acceptance. Even in modern human society, it takes a strong individual to go up against the beliefs of one's group. The individual may face all kinds of criticism, including ostracism from the group and possible physical harm if they violate the group ethos. Reason, under these circumstances, would suggest that the individual's survival depends on conforming to the desires of the group, no matter the ethical principles being displayed by the larger group at any given time. We need only look at the price individuals, who did not believe in the cause for which the nation-state in which they belonged was fighting, paid in times of war to see that "rational" action on their part may have nothing to do with morals. In fact, strong moral principles might completely get in the way of rational action when weighed against their personal or familial survival. The concept of duty then becomes a conundrum of competing interests and we can only wonder at how many soldiers felt it was easier to join the fight, even at the risk of losing their lives, rather than to refuse to fight in what they honestly felt was an unjust war. Duty to whom and to what becomes more than just an abstract academic exercise. It may be a soul-wrenching ordeal.

Morality involves the application of principles concerning the distinction between right and wrong or good and bad behavior. Here I'm trying to show that it's not just what any individual or society decides those principles to be at any given point in time, but what are the general universal precepts for behavior that appear to have evolved and held fast in all human societies down to the present. And also, those concepts of right and wrong that have antecedents in behavior not restricted to humans alone.

If we look at possible contributory behavioral factors that lead us to determine which might become a doorway to our concept of morality, we bump squarely into the practice of cooperation as a leading factor. We've already discovered that even fish can cooperate, so it's just not only in the higher animals that this trait can be found. Establishing which aspects of it might be more refined, as well as where it occurs in various species, might begin to determine a rightness or wrongness of actions.

Humans in hunter-gatherer groups like bonobos and chimps go out in food-foraging groups and cooperate in their hunt for resources. So, what's the difference between our primate cousins and us? Empathy, too, has its origins in the animal world. In his 1996 book, *The Origins of Virtue*, Matt Ridley explores the issues surrounding the development of human morality. The book is written from a sociobiological viewpoint and explores how genetics can be used to explain certain traits of human behavior, in particular morality and altruism.

Starting from the premise that society can, on a simplistic level, be represented as a variant of the prisoner's dilemma (see Appendix 1), Ridley examines how it has been possible for a society to arise in which people choose to cooperate rather than defect or forsake the group. In this meta-study, he takes a closer look at a number of computer-generated models used to explain how humans in society do not defect. He focuses particularly on systems of tit for tat, where members of the group only cooperate with those who also cooperate and exclude those who do not. This allows altruistic behavior to develop and causes the optimum solution to the dilemma: to no longer defect but instead to cooperate. He applies this to humans and suggests that genes that generated altruistic tit for tat behavior would be likely to be passed on and therefore give rise to the kind of behavior we see today. Ridley argues that society, like the largest hunter-gatherer groups, operates best in numbers of around 150 individuals. He suggests that these are numbers at which humans are capable of being sure which members they can cooperate with and which to exclude.[53]

Ethics

Socrates to contemporary philosophers have put forth their schools of thought regarding ethical values: Virtue ethics, Utilitarianism, Deontology, and more (see Appendix 2). But all depend on perspective and point of view, which, by their very nature, are subjective responses to given circumstances. In an effort to arrive at a consensus, we seem to create more theories that only further divide us. Like physicists seeking the "theory of everything" (TOE),[54] the moral quest for "the" answer always appears to beckon just beyond our reach.

Broadening the Definition of Morality

In the area of moral developmental growth, New York University social psychologist Jonathan Haidt in a 2008 article says, "The highest moral stages, which many adolescents ever reach during adolescence, require post-conventional responses, in which one goes beyond one's society and justifies rules with references to abstract and universal principles of justice."[55] I would only change Haidt's emphasis from adolescents (because adolescents' brains are not fully developed) to people in general since it only takes a brief scan of the nightly news to see adults acting like adolescents. The question becomes: Are there abstract and universal principles of justice? In an excerpt of the article, Haidt offers a new definition of morality, taking into account the many disciplines now contributing to the origins of morality, while in the entirety of the article he also explains the different philosophical and psychological schools of the past and present:

Here is my alternative approach to defining morality, written to capture the cross-disciplinary nature of the new synthesis: Moral systems are interlocking sets of values, practices, institutions, and evolved psychological mechanisms that work together to suppress or regulate selfishness and make social life possible. This is a functionalist definition that welcomes evolutionary theorists and anthropologists. It assumes that human morality arises from the co-evolution of genes and cultural innovations (Richerson & Boyd, 2005), and it assumes that cultures have found many ways to build on the broad potential of the human mind to suppress selfishness and form cooperative communities. One of those ways was laid out by John Stuart Mill and the rationalist traditions that lead up through Kohlberg. We might call it an individualist approach to morality because individuals are the fundamental units of moral value. In this approach, selfishness is suppressed by encouraging individuals to empathize with and care for the needy and vulnerable (Gilligan) and to respect the rights of others and fight for justice (Kohlberg). Authority and tradition have no value in and of themselves; they should be questioned and altered anew in each generation to suit society's changing needs. Groups also have no special value in and of themselves. People are free to form voluntary cooperatives, but we must always be vigilant against the ancient tribal instincts that lead to group-based discrimination.[56]

Here again, Haidt expresses an individual approach to morality. Just as some single-cell organisms are loners in the world of microbial life, individual human beings ultimately face themselves as carriers of moral values. This in no way diminishes the profound influence of group pressure on the individual to conform but simply reminds us that without introspection, we are indeed little more than animals following the herd. Increasing complexity in all areas of human endeavor including morality appears to be the touchstone of evolution.

Both animal minds and human minds first react intuitively to situations they encounter. That reaction is based on what will advance the individual's interest, from the "fight or flight" response to an opportunity to see a new exhibit in a museum. In the 1980s those emotional and visceral responses were discovered to be filled with cognition. In his book *Thinking Fast and Slow*, Daniel Kahneman introduces a concept he calls *System 1 and System 2*. System 1 is "fast and intuitive, and emotional." System 2 tends to be, "slower, more deliberative, and more logical."[57] It was natural for System 1 to develop first since in our hunter-gatherer days most of our time was spent just trying to survive at its most basic level. Our intuitive and emotional reactions were on high alert since life-or-death circumstances were never far from our daily lives and could turn in an instant. In System 2, our slow deliberative decision-making process, was not called for under most situations.

Haidt, in his book *The Happiness Hypothesis* discusses what he calls the elephant and rider concepts for human cognition. The elephant controls automatic processes, including emotion and intuition. The rider was developed because it did useful things for the elephant. Essentially it can see further into the future and modify some of the emotional responses of the elephant that could end up being detrimental.

Within the first second of seeing, hearing, or meeting another person, the elephant has already begun to lean toward or away, and that lean influences what we think and do next. Intuitions come first.[58] Robert Sapolsky says much the same thing, only using brain research. The amygdala takes the role of the elephant and the prefrontal cortex that of the rider.

Feeling Dirty

When people commit infractions of the moral code they believe in, they want to get clean. This is the "Macbeth effect": "out, damned spot."[59] One of the most famous biblical incidents of this behavior was that of the Roman governor of Judaea, Pontius Pilate, washing his hands after condemning Jesus, saying: "I am innocent of the blood of this just person" (Matthew 27: 24). There is a parallel in our minds about physical cleanliness and moral purity, which is hard to escape. An immoral act makes us feel "physically dirty." And the concept of a physical cleansing to wash away that moral stain is ubiquitous in culture. In Christianity you have baptism to wash away the concept of original sin. In orthodox Judaism there is the ritual bath called the mikvah in which married women, as one example, are required to bathe seven days after the end of their menstrual cycle. The circumstances may be different for different religions and cultures, but the object is the same, a ritual purification after some form of moral or physical defilement.[60] I can remember this as a young Catholic boy going to confession on Saturday afternoon and after this unburdening of my sins, I would feel that my soul was pure enough to receive Communion on Sunday morning provided I could remain pure through Saturday night.

In one strange experiment at Cornell University, which demonstrated the "cleansing effect," researchers Eri Helzer and David Pizarro had students fill out surveys indicating their political attitudes while standing near or far from a hand sanitizer dispenser. The students that stood near the hand sanitizer became temporarily more conservative. The results were found to be that when we're deciding how we think about something, we become introspective and see how we are feeling. If we feel good, we must like it. If we have an unpleasant feeling, we don't like it.[61]

If we don't like it and continue to do the deed, self-justification comes into the picture. Cognitive dissonance is the tension that exists when a person holds two psychologically inconsistent cognitions (beliefs, ideas, or attitudes) at the same time. We believe smoking is bad for us, but we smoke two packs a day. We know that eating too many desserts is causing our weight gain, but we must have that ice cream and cake after dinner. Self-justifications begin to creep up in the form of beliefs: smoking relieves tension, desserts make us feel good, etc. These are simple examples, but the human mind is complex and the machinations of one's perspective on any given circumstance know no bounds, allowing for what might, to an outsider, be absurd contradictions, but to the individual performing them, totally acceptable.[62]

The belief that people knowingly and consciously do evil acts is part of our societal mythology. It's a convenient oversimplification that allows any in-depth analysis of contributing circumstances for actions to be ignored. Each side sees itself as good and its enemy as evil. In the Second World War, the propaganda machinery was hard at work. American propaganda, for example, shows a Nazi wearing a swastika crushing a church with his boot, or the image of an arm wearing a swastika "stabbing a dagger" through the Bible. At the same time the Nazis depicted Hitler as a "Christ-like figure" or likening him to Saint George, of Christian lure slaying the evil dragon. In the propaganda poster Hitler is wearing a cross, and holding a sword to destroy a dragon, which represented "Germany's enemies."[63]

But, in a zero-sum game, it's the winners who write history and paint the losers in the worst light possible. It's not that one side is not more right than another, but generally it is the failure of reason that leads to war. Had the Allied powers after World War I treated Germany fairly in regard to war reparations would Hitler have had a chance to come to power? Had the czar and other royalty in Russia heeded the legitimate needs of the peasants and relieved their suffering prior to 1917, would Stalin have come to power? And in a tip of the hat to more contemporary history, would Donald Trump have become president of the United States had the Democrats not abandoned the working class? We cannot second-guess history, but we can probably make some assessments on the causes of conflict regarding the obvious. No one in their right mind wants to take a chance on dying in the street in a demonstration if they're leading a decent life with the necessary means to improve it if they so desire and hold the belief that the society as a whole is fair and equitable.

Problems arise when we presume to absolutely know what the greater good is and there are no counterarguments presented that force us to reconsider our positions. Certitude is the enemy of reason and the concept of a non-zero-sum game becomes impossible. War is the result on the grand scale and the dissolution of relationships on an interpersonal level. Also, in a real sense, we as individuals play alternating roles in life as the elephant or the rider. We take on a variety of positions, as the need arises, in our interactions with others. At one time, we may take more uncompromising views and, in the next, be the paragon of reason. Smart political leaders not afraid to have advisors with opposing views in their circle of counselors have a great advantage since there is the opportunity to dissuade the leader from unwise decisions. And in a democracy, this is what a checks-and-balances system among branches of government is also intended to do. Well, let's say in an ideal world, anyway, that's what it is intended.

Cultural anthropologist Margaret Mead was once asked by a student what she thought the first signs of civilization were in the anthropological record. The student believed that her answer would be something like tools, religious artifacts, hunting implements, etc. Instead, Dr. Mead said that the first real evidence of civilization was a 15,000-year-old femur bone that had been fractured and healed. It's the longest bone in the body and was found at an archeological site. Since it takes approximately six weeks to heal a fractured femur, someone had to care for the person over that period of time. An animal will not survive six weeks with a broken leg; we become a meal for the next animal that comes along. The healed femur shows that someone cared enough to nurse that individual back to health at possible risk to their own life in the process. "So, what is it about being human that makes us feel better when we help others?"[64] Is it perhaps that sense of connection to something larger than ourselves?

Summary

In Chapter 1, we saw some of the amazing discoveries that have been made in the area of understanding how different organisms meet their basic survival needs. And, how many of the seeds of the higher aspects of Maslow's Hierarchy are imbedded in those basic needs. Aspects that we formally believed were the sole domain of humans, like altruism, reciprocity, and morality, actually have their foundations in the animal world. And although brain size and gray matter still have primacy in many areas of cognitive ability, there is still so much to learn about how these other sentient beings do what they do. For those who want to explore the many mysteries of life, it's a wonderful time to be alive.

Chapter 2

Psychological Perspectives

Our investigation of physiological needs in the previous part looked at the biological processes of self-preservation and ultimately the survival of the individual as well as the species. In Chapter 2 we focus on the psychological aspects of development and how they connect to the physiological evolution of our species in particular. With that extra 2% of brain development we've moved beyond the world of chimps and bonobos to begin to see the upper layers of Maslow's Hierarchy. We now explore how our development progresses, according to leading researchers in both the social and physical sciences, and how genetics and conditioning effect the decision-making process. We also look at attitudes surrounding those decisions and examine how questions of identity affect our personal and social lives as well as our place in society. Deeper levels of self-reflection involve definitions of *ego* and *ego-self*, which are inextricably linked to our belief systems and help explain why we believe what we believe.

Heroes/Anti-heroes

When we look at the salmon that swim upstream to the spawning grounds and outlive the others, we don't view them as selfish. Rather, we view them as heroic. Or how about the one tiny sperm that out of the thousands that try is the only one who manages to survive to fertilize the female egg? "Only the strong survive" is a maxim that helps us recognize that self-preservation demands strength and that one of the best ways to survive, at least in a biological sense, is to look for a mate who is strong enough to successfully pass on our genetic material. The evolution of the overall species depends on the strongest individuals passing on their genes to the group. In the biological realm, it is most often a situation where all the gains cancel out the losses though cooperative behavior does mitigate against this. But this behavior usually exists on the grand scale, and not so much at the individual competitive level. The pecking order seems to survive from wolf packs to tribal societies.

Humans are storytellers and some of the best stories are those of heroes—individuals, who, against all odds, come out victorious. In stories, this could be the hunter feeding the tribe or the person who finds the Holy Grail. From Homer's *Odyssey* to the latest blockbuster film, these stories relate the exploits of the hero against the dark forces.

Religious histories around the world also include various heroes: Moses, Jesus, Buddha, Mohammad, the great characters from the Hindu tradition—all were marvelous individuals who met adversity and succeeded in overcoming every obstacle put in their path. In these stories, virtue conquered all. Well, at least from the perspective of the followers of those traditions.

Joseph Campbell, perhaps the most famous mythologist of the last century, has done an excellent job in his book *The Hero's Journey* describing the three stages of the path necessary for success to take place:

- Departure Act: The hero leaves the ordinary world.
- Initiation Act: The hero ventures into unknown territory (the special world) and undergoes various trials and challenges.
- Return Act: The hero returns in triumph.[65]

These three stages are the basic outline. Under each "act" are substages that describe more fully some of the processes that individuals must go through to completely realize what each stage entails. The triumph of the Return Act may not always be what one expects.

Plato's *Allegory of the Cave* is a good example of a work with all three stages: There are prisoners chained together in a cave. They can only see the wall of the cave, not the entrance. Between the prisoners is a fire that reflects light on the wall of the cave. Between the prisoners and the fire are people carrying puppets and other objects that are reflected on the wall of the cave. The prisoners can only see those reflected objects and believe them to be real. One prisoner escapes (Departure Act) and sees that the images are not real. He looks outside the cave and is amazed at all the wonders he observes in the "real" world but is temporarily blinded by the bright sunlight (Initiation Act). He returns to the cave (Return Act) and tries to explain to the other prisoners that what they see on the wall is an illusion, but the prisoners seeing his blindness believe if they leave the cave they will be harmed. Consequently, his triumphal return is compromised by fear.

All that said, we probably would be hard pressed to find any popular or ancient hero myth that did not encompass all three stages. Luke Skywalker in Star Wars, Dorothy in the Wizard of Oz, and countless other hero stories including the lives of major religious leaders like Buddha and Jesus, all follow the same template though the specifics of each are unique. As Joseph Campbell has said, we must find our own entrance into the forest. It is our specific path to discover.

True heroism is rare because it is difficult and although we see many instances of individual heroic behavior, such as when ordinary people save others in a spontaneous moment, it is far from the norm. Not everyone can meet the challenges that transform the person from the ordinary to the consistently exceptional. Yet, still, we hold out the hero as the model, the exemplar of what we should become. If we do not attain the status of hero, we tend to vicariously live through others who do. The sports hero, the war hero, astronauts, great artists, business moguls as well as the Martin Luther Kings and Mother Teresas of the world all have their place in the pantheon of those we anoint as heroes. We want to be like them and, if not like them, then to at least embody some of their fine qualities.

Sometimes, though, we prefer to be the anti-hero. "Better to reign in hell than serve in heaven," said Lucifer in John Milton's *Paradise Lost*.[66] We need not go that far, of course, but there is a dark side of the human personality that is tempting. Human beings are, after all, both among the most violent of species as well as among the most altruistic and compassionate. The renegade, outlaw, or pirate, all have their particular bad guy allure.

Even in childhood. How many kids dress up as pirates or Darth Vader from Star Wars on Halloween? The costume shops never seem to tire of making new outfits for the bad guys. One of the later examples of pirates would probably be the Captain Jack Sparrow character from *Pirates of the Caribbean* and before that there was Long John Silver, the pegleg pirate captain from Robert Lewis Stevenson's *Treasure Island*. The list of bad guys we love to hate includes not only males but femme fatale characters as well: Cleopatra, Jezebel, and Delilah in the ancient world, and although not as famous as the male scoundrels, the world of cinema is beginning to produce more female characters in this mode, Catwoman and Maleficent, for example.

We all have a dark side: those traits we are ashamed of and embarrassed about. As author Heidi Priebe put it, "We hate anti-heroes in part because we're scared that we are exactly like them—Flawed. Immoral. Lost. We don't want to recognize the parts of ourselves that resemble these complicated characters because we'd rather be the heroes."[67]

Rebellion against the natural or imposed order has a long history: the rebellion of Adam and Eve against God by eating the forbidden fruit is certainly one of the great archetypes. But as Adam and Eve found out, do we know the benefit of good if we do not know evil?

Our lizard or reptilian brain loves to divide the world into perceived right and wrong, and most of the time "we" are right and "they" are wrong. Once we have cast ourselves as the one who is right and them as wrong all sorts of things can be justified. The Stanford Prison Experiment of 1971 is cited as evidence of the atavistic impulses that lurk within us all, suggesting that, with a little nudge, we could all become tyrants. In the study, college students were chosen to re-create a prison setting. They were all required to answer a "questionnaire" regarding family and medical history, including physical and mental health. Social behavior was also assessed. A flip of a coin determined who would become the "guards" versus the "prisoners." The guards were provided with very little instruction on how to treat the prisoners. Very quickly, they began "humiliating and psychologically abusing" the prisoners. The prisoners became "submissive and depersonalized" in the process and did little to protest their treatment. The researchers were so surprised by the early results that the planned two-week experiment was cut short after only six days.[68]

On the other end of the spectrum, we have the example of the Christmas Truce of 1914 during the First World War when soldiers decided to disobey orders. On December 7, 1914, Pope Benedict XV suggested a temporary truce for the celebration of Christmas and although the warring countries refused any official ceasefire, the troops themselves declared their own unofficial truce. Starting on Christmas Eve and lasting through Christmas Day, German and British troops abandoned their trenches and went out into the no-man's land to retrieve their dead comrades. They also sang carols and greeted their enemies with gifts and handshakes and sang carols together. Some who survived recalled that it was a celebration of love that brought mortal enemies together. Who knows if had it not been for their officers threatening disciplinary action to the point of shooting their own men for disobedience, the event may have gone on to do something to end the war earlier.[69]

We seem to love the extremes of all good or all bad, the devil on one shoulder, the angel on the other. Dualism pervades our thinking. However, outside of movie theaters and fiction novels, life is not like that. We live most of the time in the gray areas. There are no one-dimensional characters in real life. And to the entertainment industry's credit, the most interesting movie and TV dramas have made plots and characters far more multi-dimensional today than in decades past. Maleficent comes to mind in the newer Disney film version of the Sleeping Beauty story. It's just harder to completely dislike her. She's had her problems and at some level we can relate to her. Moral ambiguity, even in the villain, is more pronounced today. Perhaps it's because the more we learn about the functioning of the brain the less certain we are of what causes particular types of behavior. And that understanding is beginning to manifest itself in art and literature. The artist exposes this flirtation with the dark side of our characters. While hiding behind the costume mask as a child or the mask of personality as an adult, we often deny this part of ourselves to our detriment. Our dark sides are part of who we are. By uncovering and embracing our shadow side, we become whole.

When we dig into the backgrounds of these heroes and villains, often seminal incidents arise to help us understand what made them do what they did. In the case of the anti-hero, it may have been childhood abuse or a negative environment. Can a child who has been physically abused during all their formative years be expected to be kind and loving toward others? Abandonment issues may challenge victims decades after the incident that caused it, and unless effectively dealt with, create problems for them for the rest of their lives. In extreme cases a pathological genetic proclivity may go awry (let's put Hitler in that group for a moment). Now conversely, for the hero, it may have been exceptionally gifted parenting, good genes, or conditioning that allowed them to overcome obstacles and successfully come out on top, as in Campbell's *Hero's Journey*.

Moral decisions, more often than not, are nuanced and difficult and if we don't take the time to think, the elephant, not the rider, runs the show, which in some ways is not unlike evolution itself. Just as brain development prioritized the amygdala first, since it dealt with the first orders of survival (food, water shelter, protection, etc.) in order to give us those early survival fundamental benefits as priorities, the later development of the prefrontal cortex aided us as our environment became increasingly complex. No longer are things strictly black and white or good or evil. The more we find out about any given situation, the more complex the moral circumstances we uncover. And as Shakespeare's Hamlet said, "There is nothing that is either good or bad, but thinking makes it so."

That's hard to accept. How can simply thinking make something good or bad? Isn't there an objective moral truth about actions and even thoughts?[70]

We *can* all accept the ordinary highs and lows of life, living most of our existence in the proverbial middle ground of the emotional spectrum, but it's only through the admission that we all have the extremes in us that we can truly understand ourselves and others. This recognition and acceptance allows us to connect with both the villain and the saint. It doesn't mean that cause and effect ceases, or that there should be no consequence for actions.

A fundamental misunderstanding regarding Maslow's Hierarchy is that once a lower need is met, we can just forget about it and focus on the next. If the current coronavirus pandemic teaches us anything, it is that the lower survival needs are never very far from our door. Rather, the needs are congruent, and as one need in the hierarchy is met, the major focus of attention becomes concentrated on the next. But just because the lower need has been met for the present doesn't mean it will continue to be met in the future. Our focus may change, given the circumstances we face. Health issues, for example, may quickly divert our attention from our careers to basic physiological survivability. And the need for esteem may be interrupted by family issues.

There is a Zen story that dramatically illustrates these circumstances. After listening to the complaints of a student who was having some psychological problems, the Zen teacher promptly gave the student a hard slap across the face. There's nothing like physical pain to block out psychological pain. It is, to be sure, a temporary fix for the individual's state of mind and one intended to bring the student back to the present moment. The object lesson of the exercise is either learned or not depending on the self-awareness of the student and timing by the teacher. Zen tends to be one of the more rigorous approaches to the practice of mindfulness and not a practice casually entered into. But more on this subject later in the book.

What and who is the "I" or "me" that the focus of attention is most particularly upon? People often say that the search for meaning or purpose is the most important aspect of their lives. But is that really true? Are meaning and purpose just subcategories sitting underneath the fundamental question of "Who am I?" After all, who is the "I" that needs a purpose beyond simply existing? Is the "I" unique to humans? Certainly, at least as far as we know, animals don't reflect on their existence. The history of philosophy, on the other hand, certainly shows that self-reflection has taken up a great deal of our time.

The Self

Both Eastern and Western philosophy have long been concerned with the study of "self." In the West, it later branched off and developed into psychology, save the area of philosophy called "Philosophy of Mind."[71] So, what is the self that consumes so much of the time and effort of philosophers and scientists, and is that the "me" that must survive? The fact is we simply don't know; at least not in any definitive sense. There is no universal agreement on what the self is. Our opinions exist in belief silos, one group claiming to know categorically what it is from one perspective and other groups saying no, not true from their perspective. The discussions run the gamut from the purely biological belief that self belongs to the natural world and is essentially materialistic in that it is the total of our evolutionary state of being, to the spiritual idea that it is something like a soul that transcends the limits of space, time, and matter. And in the words of Carl Jung: "As an empirical concept, the self designates the whole range of psychic phenomena in man. It expresses the unity of the personality as a whole."[72] Jung also says, "The self is not only the centre, but also the whole circumference which embraces both conscious and unconsciousness; it is the centre of this totality."[73]

Putting aside the various definitions of self for the time being, in this portion of the book we're going to look at the subject of self from a more common perspective—the "I" that thinks, feels, and acts in the world. This I may be restrictive or expansive, depending on the individual, but at this point we will simply refer to it as the *ego-self*. In general, this view of self is closer to a Freudian take.[74] And, in its most basic understanding, it is the "I" that we carry around with us most of the time and refer to when speaking of ourselves. When we think of this idea of the self, it most often has to do with memory. We remember who we are. The English philosopher John Locke, for example, considered memory to be the foundation of identity. He wrote in 1694 that consciousness always accompanies thinking. And if we traced our memories backward, we always were the central part of those memories. This idea of self seems to even persist with brain injuries that cause amnesia and another condition called *anterograde amnesia*, which prevents new memories from forming. Even in these cases, the sense of self is not lost.[75]

Psychology

Philosophy birthed psychology as a separate discipline in the 1800s and although we can say that philosophy has been the study of the mind for thousands of years, the particular methodologies of psychology were not developed until this later period. The discipline began with German physiologist Wilhelm Wundt, who was using scientific research methods to investigate reaction times. He published a book called *Principles of Physiological Psychology* in 1873 that outlined the major connections between the science of physiology and the study of human thought and behavior. His work later developed into psychology, which became a separate discipline. Wundt saw psychology as the study of human consciousness and examined how experimental methods could be used to look at internal mental processes. And, although his use of a process he defined as "introspection" is not deemed reliable today, it set the stage for much of the methodology used in psychological practice.

Like all of the scientific fields that are becoming more complex and even spawning new discrete scientific disciplines, so, too, is psychology; putting strict boundaries around these disciplines is becoming increasingly more difficult. Cognitive psychology, which developed in the 1950s and '60s, for example, studies areas such as perception, memory, decision-making, problem-solving, intelligence, and language. It now uses tools like MRI and PET scans to help understand the workings of the human brain. This, of course, bumps into the field of neuroscience. Again, the edges of disciplines are continually overlapping, requiring scientists to be both more aware of research done in other areas and to have a greater acceptance concerning the interconnectedness of all the pertinent scientific disciplines.[76]

Needs

When we talk about Maslow's Hierarchy of motivational needs, we need to ask the question, to what end? The pleasure principle plays a role: The desire to seek pleasure and avoid pain is fundamental. But the belief that attaining the goals we chase will make us happy remains, once achieved, a temporary state of being. The feeling of discontent after achieving any given level of well-being and recognizing that there is something more is the itch that must be scratched. So much so that, although all of the needs exist in service to the individual's desire to survive, they do so at increasingly higher levels of complexity. Survival no longer means just to live but to transcend.

Ego

Ego in Latin means "I." Merriam-Webster defines *ego* as "the self especially as contrasted with another self or the world."[77] It is this separate self with which we are most concerned. This does not in any way exclude the biological associations of self. This "I" still includes concepts of altruism, cooperation, and self-sacrifice, which are merely extensions of the ego-self from a personal perspective interacting with the environment. *Me* and *mine* relate to everything I consider mine, from objects to families to tribal associations. This is generally reinforced by societal norms, even though different political systems may weigh the balance of individualism and communalism differently. Ultimately, we're speaking of individuals who manifest those ego needs most strongly, independent of the political system of which they are members.

Sigmund Freud popularized the term "ego" and it has become part of the common language. Context is important and it may be helpful to review a few of Freud's beliefs concerning the place of the ego in the human psyche. Freud believed human personality was "very complex" and was made up of the following components: "the id, the ego and the superego." They are the elements of human personality and are integrated in working together in creating "complex human behaviors."[78]

He also believed that the id is the only component present

from birth and is essentially instinctive and primal. The id works on the pleasure principle and strives for immediate gratification. If that gratification is not fulfilled, anxiety and tension result. An infant experiencing hunger or thirst, for example, will cry until its needs are met. Trying to reason with an infant to calm it down is out of the question if food or drink are not readily available.

As we grow, the ego develops from the id. We gradually begin to understand that all of our instinctual needs cannot be met when we would like. Societal norms come into play and we begin to learn concepts like delayed gratification. The ego-self learns to wait for the right time and place. Reciprocity also begins to play a role. Our behavior, in other words, begins to adapt to the norms of the greater society and influences our perception of reality. Some researchers say that this is the real beginning of morality, which also exists in the animal world, particularly in primates.[79]

Freud believed the superego begins to emerge around age five, although he was probably off by a couple of years, since the frontal lobes don't develop until about age seven, when we begin to see those moral standards and ideals acquired from our parents and society come into being.[80] The rights and wrongs that become the basis of our moral understanding are developed during this time. According to Freud, the superego forms our outlines for making judgments. It includes the development of conscience, the source of judgments regarding what's good and bad, as well as our feelings about guilt, punishment, and remorse.[81] It's interesting that in some religious systems, the age of reason is considered to be seven, as is the case with the Roman Catholic Church, at which time the child may also receive Communion. Some evangelical churches also attribute seven as the age a child is old enough to make independent spiritual choices. In both Judaism and Islam, a boy of seven begins religious studies and begins to participate to some degree in rituals.[82] In all of these cases, responsibility for one's actions is formally introduced to the child.

Freud believed that the key to a healthy personality is a balance between the id, ego, and superego. So, a person who has good "ego strength" would refer to a person who could effectively balance and manage the pressures of the competing forces of the id and superego. Conversely, one that could not adequately balance these forces might develop a maladaptive personality.[83]

The Brain

We now know that the amygdala is fully developed at birth (as Freud said of the id) and possesses all the fundamental self-preservation drives. Maturation plays a role, but we might say that in the first level of Maslow's Hierarchy, those needs grouped under "physiological needs," meaning those that can be satisfied externally (i.e., food shelter clothing, safety etc.), are encompassed in the amygdala. The modifying principles that control the basic survival urges are developed in the prefrontal cortex, which begins development in early childhood but is not complete until the late twenties, particularly in men. This is possibly one reason violent crime and risky behavior dramatically drop after age thirty for men and much earlier for women whose prefrontal cortex develops more quickly. A girl's body also matures more quickly than a boy's and goes through puberty up to two years faster than boys. The reason for this faster development is probably related to child-rearing responsibilities for women.[84]

Yet, those feelings of self-righteous indignation often stem from the amygdala, not the prefrontal cortex. We most often don't think of all the causes for others' decisions, but instead make snap judgments about those decisions based on our feelings. We don't make moral judgments by simply weighing harms and benefits in a rational way. That takes time. It's a more immediate process similar to what animals do as they negotiate their environment. They feel drawn toward or away from things, and that judgment is done for the most part by the elephant.[85] One could imagine being a member of a hunter-gatherer group going through the jungle and suddenly being confronted by a lion. Thinking about it for more than a couple of seconds might mean becoming dinner for the lion. In our own lives, if we see a crime being committed, especially if it appears to be against a defenseless person, we make snap judgments regarding the morality of the incident we are witnessing.

Perception

Perception is how we view the world and ourselves. To observe, identify, label, and name becomes our "truth," at least temporarily. On the other hand, reality is not out there, apart from our mind. Our mind is part of reality. And what we observe as reality is in some sense an illusion, because it is subjectively interpreted by us. We are like reality observing itself, but only one interpretation of reality.

Our perception is not all that there is. And, in fact, our perception is only a tiny fraction of all that there is. Any interpretation we might have of reality can only be partial. We are prone to error and there is a barrier between our subjective experience of reality and the nature of reality itself.[86]

But is there truly an objective reality or do we construct reality? Is what we believe we know and what we don't know now so comingled that making categorical statements about the nature of reality is too complicated? In philosophy and science today the subject of reality, and whether we know objectively what it is, has become a major question for both fields. However, most laypersons and nonprofessionals have no such problems regarding such discussions. In most minds, 2 + 2 always equals 4. Thus, basic math proves the existence of objective truth. It makes sense and arguing with someone about the possibility that it may not always be true is generally a useless pursuit. Discussions of right and wrong often follow the same trajectory. But some things are true at one level of understanding, but not necessarily so under another set of circumstances. Even in mathematics the 2 + 2 = 4 examples, once removed from the abstraction of numbers and brought into the world of things, are not true in every circumstance. We usually say that if we add two quarts of water to two quarts of water we get four quarts, but if we take that same example into a laboratory and measure those quarts of water scientifically, we see that some evaporation will occur and the answer is no longer four. It might not matter much to a recipe in the kitchen, but it might matter a great deal in a scientific experiment, especially using other sources, radioactive material, for example. If a critical mass is exceeded it might add up to a whole lot more than four.[87]

There are many more complex examples, but you get the point. Understanding concepts is oftentimes situational and restricted to a given set of circumstances. A common understanding is just that—common. As we move along the continuum from simple to complex, we must constantly be aware of our environment. Survival in a hunter-gatherer tribe is not the same as surviving on Wall Street, even if some of the motivations for acting may be similar. A high level of interpersonal skills or, as Howard Gardner says, *interpersonal intelligence,* allows those people who possess it to maneuver easily in many different social environments;[88] those with lesser ability, however, find it extremely difficult to feel comfortable when changing their familiar social circumstances. But even with this skill set, don't we all feel somewhat out of place when the circumstances in which we find ourselves are foreign to us? This could be because of a different language, culture, or any number of things—particularly if it goes on over an extended time—which then begins to threaten our sense of comfort and well-being.

In a dimly lit room, a curled rope might resemble a snake, and if the room is unfamiliar to us and is located in an area where snakes are known to be present, the rope may look even more like a snake. Perception is all we have and how our minds play with that faculty determines our state of mind and often our beliefs.

Objectivity

In a recent study at Johns Hopkins University, researchers tested a longstanding philosophical question: Can people see the world objectively? The lead researcher on the study, a neuroscientist with a doctorate in philosophy, discovered through a series of experiments using laser-cut "coins," and sophisticated computer graphics, it's almost impossible for people to separate an object's true identity from their perspective on it. For example, even when people were certain that objects were round, if the object was tilted away from them, they saw them as "ovals or ellipses." According to the Johns Hopkins team, true objective vision is impossible. It appears that when the truth depends on our perception, objectivity takes a back seat.[89] One of the great narrative films on the subject was Akira Kurosawa's 1950 film *Rashomon*, in which four different witnesses who were influenced by their own life experiences describe a murder in four contradictory ways.

Perhaps it should be no surprise, then, that so many philosophers today also have degrees in neuroscience, since it's only with today's technology and science that we can more deeply investigate some of the questions that have perplexed humanity for centuries. With some of these questions being answered we, of course, discover other questions we had previously never even thought of asking.

Ladder of Inference: One View of the Decision-Making Process

The ladder of inference is a metaphorical thinking model first proposed by Chris Argyris (1923–2013) in 1970. Argyris was a professor at the Harvard Business School. The ladder is a way of describing how one moves from a piece of data—be it a comment made, something read, or something observed to have happened—through a series of mental processes to a conclusion. The "rungs" of the ladder are the specific mental steps we take on our way to taking action based on our understanding. The difficulty in negotiating each rung is with our perception.

Starting bottom-up we'll take a look at each rung on the ladder:

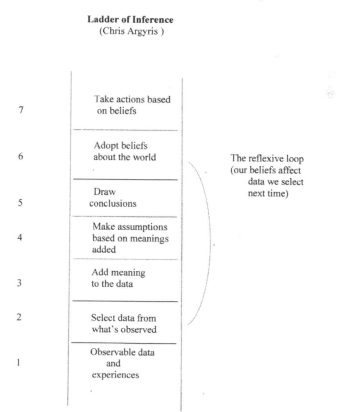

Ladder of Inference
(Chris Argyris)

7	Take actions based on beliefs
6	Adopt beliefs about the world
5	Draw conclusions
4	Make assumptions based on meanings added
3	Add meaning to the data
2	Select data from what's observed
1	Observable data and experiences

The reflexive loop (our beliefs affect data we select next time)

Step 1. Observe data.
Looking at observable data as a video camera with no preference or bias toward anything in view

Step 2. Select data.
Based on perception, selecting data perceived as most important

Step 3. Add meaning to the data.
Assigning meaning to the data based on life experiences, biases, and beliefs

Step 4. Make assumptions based on meaning.
Making assumptions based on assigned meaning, which in turn allows one to ignore the other factors that may be present

Step 5. Draw conclusions.
Drawing conclusions based on our assumptions

Step 6. Adopt beliefs based on conclusions.
Adopting beliefs based on conclusions drawn and using to shape future judgments

Step 7. Take action.
Taking action based on beliefs and assumptions, which may or may not be based on facts

There is a reflexive loop that happens between steps 2 and 6, when we adopt beliefs and conclusions for those beliefs at level 6, which are based on life experiences. They tend to interfere with any possible "objective" view of observed data at level 1. Our biases have already been created by our past experiences and therefore color anything we see. We no longer can have an objective view of the "data" and are preconditioned to select data at level 2. That is the overall problem with perception.

Because it is subjective, we end up struggling with all of our preconditioning, making it more difficult to be more open to experiences that may contradict our preconditioned beliefs.[90] It's easy to just say, use the ladder of inference to make better decisions.[91] But we make judgments based on our biases that may go back to epigenetic influences or our tribal associations, let alone personal experience.

Let's take one example: We're invited to a co-worker's wedding. He is from a different racial group. We don't think much of it until we get to the wedding, when we discover that we are the only member of a different racial group than the rest of the people at the wedding. What goes through our head? People are friendly to us but we can't help feeling what we are feeling. Can we, in an objective way, analyze those feelings, or do they just rush in and take over our thought process? Can we really try to be objective in the step 1 phase of the ladder of inference? Probably not. At least not unless we have been "the only one" on so many occasions that we now have a good handle on our biased feelings and have taken the time and effort to deal with those feelings. Our emotions are in play and the process we must go through is one of reconditioning, and that takes repetition, time, and an adjustment in perception. Hence Marcel Proust's saying, "The real voyage of discovery consists not in seeking new landscapes, but in having new eyes." Thankfully, the plasticity of the brain allows for this to happen, but more on this later.

Identity plays a major role in this drama and we've discussed to some degree the concept of the self. How that self-identity is constructed depends on our life circumstances, both intra-personally with our perception of ourselves and interpersonally with our interaction with society (including family) and the effects they have on us, which in turn mold our self-image. We can't help but be conditioned by our experiences and we are hardwired to do so. Just think about amoebas. Without a brain or a nervous system they were conditioned by their experiences to do amazing things. That sense of self (not necessarily meaning self-aware) is above all what needs to survive and adjust to our environment and is what is needed to do so.

Free Will

Volition, control, or what we call free will to choose is integral to our notion of self. The belief that we can make choices is profoundly important to both personal and societal well-being.[92] It's no mystery why people want to believe in free will. The concept reinforces our sense of self and those who feel that they have little control over their lives or perceive that they have little control suffer from some of the highest rates of depression.[93]

Philosophers have been debating the concept of free will for millennia, but now neuroscientists have joined in on the melee. In an attempt to get everyone on the same page, the first intensive research collaboration between neuroscientists and philosophers, backed by a $7 million grant from two private foundations, the John Templeton Foundation and the Fetzer Institute, took place at an inaugural conference in March 2019. Attendees discussed plans for designing philosophically informed experiments and unanimously agreed on the need to pin down the various meanings of "free will." The new research program involves neuroscientists and philosophers from seventeen universities working over a four-year period to try and solve this puzzle.[94]

The neuroscientists and philosophers aim to jostle with the question of free will for some time. They will work on what questions to start asking about its existence or nonexistence and exactly what we mean when we say *free will*. But for now, we can ask: Is the common idea of free will compatible with what we have just illustrated above with the ladder of inference? Is it a question of having free will or not having it? Do we possibly have some partial free will, like a veneer laid on top of a block of conditioning and genetic proclivities? Don't we feel we are making choices? What about intention, intuition, and deliberative decision-making?

Well, at least to a growing number of biologists and neuroscientists the answer is that we probably don't have what we commonly refer to as free will. One famous study showed that before we decide to move, there's already brain activity preparing for that move three hundred milliseconds earlier. The body was preparing to move even before we consciously wanted to move.[95] The experiment has been duplicated with similar results. A 2008 study also found that brain activity measuring the onset of conscious motor intentions occurred up to ten seconds ahead of conscious awareness of making a decision.[96] Speaking on this point, philosopher and neuroscientist Sam Harris writes:

One fact now seems indisputable: Some moments before you are aware of what you will do next—a time in which you subjectively appear to have complete freedom to behave however you please—your brain has already determined what you will do. You then become conscious of this decision and believe that you are in the process of making it. You are not controlling the storm, and you are not lost in it. You are the storm.[97]

So, for Sam Harris and many other scientists, we do not choose our thoughts or feelings, but just become consciously aware of them.

Physicist Brian Green discounts the idea of free will altogether, stating "thoughts and actions are simply interactions between elementary particles, which are bound to obey mathematical equations," but he goes on to say, "and yet even in that environment our particular arrangements can, through a flitting burst of activity, create beauty, illuminate mystery, experience wonder.... The fact that particles can do that fills me with a sense of gratitude that borders on reverence."[98] This is a humble position Green is expressing here, but most of us still cling to the feeling and need for autonomy. It's important to believe that "we" are making the decisions.

From another point of view in favor of free will, what about when we become aware of the decision and are about to carry it out? Do we have the ability to change our minds? Isn't the belief that we could have done otherwise under similar or the same conditions important? This argument infers an independent and objective chooser, a self that can be found somewhere in our head that is objective. Thus far our best science cannot find where in our brain this self resides, or if that sense of self exists outside of our experiences. The concept that the "self" is localized to a particular area of the brain is contradicted by scientific research. It rather extends to a "broad range of fluctuating neural processes" that do not appear to be localized.[99] Evidently, neither science or even Buddhism for that matter, believe in an unchanging self. Rather, that in both science and Buddhism the concept of the "self" is ever changing over time.[100] Therefore, isn't it more likely that the idea of changing one's mind would still have nothing to do with free will? The thought of changing one's mind would just start the neuronal chain of events over again and we're back to the ladder of inference and our conditioning. The most infinitesimal change in anything could affect another causal chain. Neuroscience does not give final answers, at least not yet. Even Libet, the person who did one of the most famous experiments against free will, wrote in 2004, "Given the issue is so fundamentally important to our view of who we are, a claim that our free will is illusory should be based on fairly direct evidence.... Such evidence is not available."[101]

The concept of self is inextricably linked to the subject of consciousness and that, according to most philosophers and neuroscientists today, is the real frontier to investigate. More on the subject of consciousness in the next chapter, but let's continue for a bit on free will. How does this belief or disbelief in free will play out in the real world?

We've depended on the belief that people are responsible for their actions and live in a world where justice systems have relied on personal responsibility to give a sense of order to society. In one study, people in a control group were instructed to read an article by Nobel Laureate Francis Crick, claiming that who we are is nothing but a pack of neurons and that our behavior is determined. The study went on to say that although we appear to have free will our choices have been predetermined and we can't change that. After that, the participants, along with a control group who had not read the article against free will, were instructed to take a twenty-problem arithmetic test. A "fake" computer glitch in the program allowed participants to see the answers if they chose to do so, but they were "on their honor" not to do so. They were told that no one would know if they looked at the answers, but they were asked not to cheat. The results showed that those that had read the article against free will cheated more than the control group that did not read the article.[102]

If we follow this reasoning out, we can't help but accept that if people did not believe in free will, they would, in general, behave more unethically and more selfishly. The personal pleasure principle would make more sense in a deterministic universe. But is that really so? It turns out that even people who "explicitly deny free will" most often hold themselves responsible for their actions and feel guilty when they do wrong. Is this just a hangover of societal conditioning or is something more going on?[103] Will some people obey societal rules without external constraints and consequences and, if so, why so? There are those working on the pleasure principle that ask, "Why should I obey laws if I'm not held accountable for my actions?", and it seems logical to assume that without consequences many people will cheat in any number of ways, using all kinds of justifications for doing so to derive some personal benefit.

In a recent study, researchers found that cheating is common, but what was more surprising was that in one experiment people who cheated believed that they knew the answers to test questions all along, which served as a disconnect in their moral perception of themselves. Rather than admit that they had cheated, they just claimed that they really knew the answers to the questions on which they had cheated.[104] Recent research shows that we are very likely to lie to ourselves concerning who we are and how we behave. The tendency is to distance ourselves from our past mistakes and in many cases just forget them altogether. Instead, we tend to see ourselves as becoming increasingly moral over time.[105] Self-protection appears to be the default action here. Once again, our perception blinds us to reality, since our ego survival is our prime motivator.

It would seem here that self-deception and narcissism become survival mechanisms without which our own self-perception may look impossibly bleak.[106] If in retrospect we can make ourselves more moral than we are, doesn't that add to our ego-sense of self-righteousness and superiority? If that's so, do we then have an ego need to believe in free will?

Chance, Choice, or Destiny

When we look back over the trajectory of our lives, it's sometimes tempting to speculate on the forces that have shaped the directions we have taken. Did we really make all those choices? Was there something at play that we were simply unaware of or was it all simply cause and effect? Could a soothsayer look at the seeds implanted in our past and predict our future with some degree of accuracy? While it's not within the purview of this book to ask those questions, I will, however, relate a personal story that gives me pause and prevents me from being categorical in considering any judgments in this area.

In 1987, I was teaching in a very large junior high school in the Oakland Hills in California. It was an upper middle-class school with an enormous music program. I taught 275 students a day in five classes of band and orchestra. The largest class was advanced band, which had a total of 90 students. My frustration in this job was not only due to a large number of students — because there were so many, I could never remember all of their names nor even get to know them all by the end of the school year. At the same time, and despite the heavy workload, I was trying to maintain a professional playing career, at least on weekends.

Several years earlier and before I took this job, my wife and I joined a yoga meditation group. It happened that Carlos Santana and his wife, Deborah, were also members of this group. We got to know each other and, during the time I was teaching at this particular school, the drummer in Carlos's band decided to leave the group. I knew that Carlos was looking for a drummer at the time and I decided I would audition for his band. I wanted desperately to go back to playing music for a living and particularly to get away from teaching in this hectic environment. So, one day I found myself at Carlos and Deborah's house in Marin County California playing with Carlos in his studio. For whatever reason, Carlos did not pick me to play in his band, maybe I simply was not as good as I thought I was; I don't know, but the rejection put me in a funk and made working at my teaching job even more frustrating. Here, however, the saying — when one door closes, another opens — is an appropriate aphorism. Just fifteen minutes from my home, the San Francisco School of the Arts High School had an opening for a music director. I interviewed and was accepted for the job. It was a wonderful teaching position, with dedicated students, a talented faculty, and was also close to my house, instead of the hour-plus commute across the San Francisco–Oakland Bay Bridge.

The job change caused a profound difference in my attitude, and although I still loved playing music, teaching was now giving me a great deal of joy. Getting to know students, since the numbers were much smaller, was incredibly satisfying. When we realize we are making a positive difference in someone's life, we typically are much happier people.

Irony, however, has a habit of poking its head up in unusual ways. A few years after starting my new job at the School of the Arts, Santana's son, Salvador, auditioned for the band in our school. Admission to the school was conditional on passing the entrance audition in one of the six arts disciplines taught at the school. After passing the audition, Salvador became a well-loved member of the band, Carlos became a frequent visitor to the school, and his wife, Deborah, volunteered at many school events. He even did a fundraising concert to help out our school. In his son's final year, Carlos and two of his band members were featured playing in the spring concert with our school orchestra at the Fillmore Auditorium, one of the venues where he began his career during the 1960s.

So, although I didn't get a chance to play in his band, he got to play in my orchestra and in the process helped hundreds of students fulfill their dreams. Instead of being a drummer in a top Latin Rock band, I became a conductor of a wonderful high school orchestra. Instead of being on the road touring for six to eight months of the year, away from my family, I got to watch my children grow up and be part of the lives of hundreds of wonderful young people, many of whom are now members of symphony orchestras around the world. And I'm lucky enough to call many of them my friends. Chance, choice, or destiny—I just don't know, but in retrospect, I'm very happy with the way it turned out.

Chapter 2

Manipulation

Another reason to reject the argument against free will is our aversion to manipulation. The idea that we are just puppets being manipulated by causal forces goes against the grain of our sense of autonomy and independence. However, when we look at manipulation in a broad sense, don't we all participate in the game? Earlier, we saw that all organic life forms struggle as they compete for resources. They compete for dominance in a hierarchy for resources to reproduce and survive. Most animals from viruses to tigers cloak or disguise themselves to avoid being detected, whether to avoid becoming prey or to become a more successful predator. We humans do much the same but use more sophisticated methods, which may be cruel or kind, depending on what we want.[107]

In our world, we don't call education manipulation because we are doing it for the good of the child, but how much of that is relative to our point of view? When we trace the history of education, we see that it is full of practices that promote the utilitarian needs of society, which may not necessarily be for the overall good and well-being of children. One practice that still lingers in some school districts is the practice of "tracking." Starting in the 1930s, it was common practice to track children in public schools according to their perceived achievement level, with little regard to what course preferences the children had. The practice became more controversial in later years because it proved particularly discriminatory to minority students. Although the practice may have some merits, society does, after all, need a variety of skilled workers, it gives little choice over one's educational opportunities to the student or parent.

Childrearing itself is full of manipulative practices, with fear being a mainstay of control. Don't do X or Y will happen. Concerning religious and political education, how fine is the line between education and indoctrination? There is much in the Abrahamic religions filled with the threat of severe repercussions. "You will go to hell if you do that." In a capitalistic society, "socialism is evil." If we're in a socialist society, "capitalism is evil." How much advertising is manipulative? "If we buy this new car, we will be more attractive to that person of the opposite sex." We are constantly told through every medium what material object we need in order to be happy. What about the clever argument? Even when we believe we are being honest in a discussion, is the underlying motivation simply one way of gaining an advantage to promote our point of view? And, although we praise the ability to think critically, is that process also conditioned by the ladder of inference and personal bias?

Conditioning today has reached new heights never before envisioned, both for good and bad, with social media being perhaps the most powerful influence humans have ever invented. In a recent documentary titled *Social Dilemma*, former employees of major companies such as Facebook, Google, Apple, and others decided that what they knew about the negative effects and motivations of these companies had to be exposed. The result was a shocking exposé of the methods used to control and influence our thinking and actions in almost every area of our lives. And because we depend so heavily on these devices and the fact that their use is so addictive, letting go of them is akin to overcoming a drug habit. As they point out in the film, the customer, as in the case of the drug customer, is called a "user." Since these companies track just about everything we do, from the websites we visit to the products we buy, their knowledge of us is beyond what we can imagine. We labor under the belief that we are using these devices in an autonomy bubble when, in fact, the companies know our every move. And because they already know what we like, they direct us to products and services they know appeal to us.

Even areas we feel are simply subjects of our research are influenced by the questions we ask. For example, if we google *climate change*, the search algorithms consider our backgrounds and then send us definitions that comport with our beliefs. That process skews our understanding, thinking that others googling the same thing will get the same answers, thus leading to even further polarization when we try to discuss the subject with those who may have different opinions. Finally, does the illusion of autonomy become an accepted substitute for autonomy itself, if indeed true autonomy exists at all? And just because we can't see the strings, does it mean we're not being manipulated?

Thoughts

Where do they come from? Do we choose them? Obviously not.[108] They pop into our head uninvited and often unwanted. Can we control which thoughts come into our minds? Again, obviously not. At best, we can choose which thoughts to focus on or let go of so that process, we might say, becomes an afterthought when it enters the realm of our conscious awareness.[109]

So, where is the free will when it comes to which thoughts we allow to come into our minds? The best we can do is not give them energy or focus if we don't want them. Hopefully they then eventually tire of not getting attention and move on to be replaced by other uninvited thoughts, perhaps ones that are more to our liking. Concentration will allow us to focus on the subject at hand and, depending on our powers of concentration, may give us extended periods when we can hold unwanted thoughts at bay. Numerous meditation techniques give hints as to how to condition ourselves so that the unwanted thoughts will have less power or that the process of meditation itself will give us the best chance of minimizing the influence of unwanted thoughts that come into our minds. But, to simply say, "I'm not going to think of X, Y, or Z," well, good luck with that one.

Willpower

And what of willpower? We all have a will, strong or weak. The question is: how free is it, if at all? People with a strong will get things done. They can be single-minded in the directionality of their focus and attention. They can lose weight, quit smoking, or start a company. They can also create an elaborate Ponzi scheme, start a war, or rob a bank. The point is when they put their mind to something, stuff happens. A weak-willed person, on the other hand, is usually a procrastinator. "Don't do today what we can put off until tomorrow." And when it comes to temptation for such weak-willed folks, Oscar Wilde famously said, "The only way to get rid of a temptation is to yield to it."

Willpower is put on the back burner. But how much is willpower itself a product of environment and conditioning? We know that the ability to delay gratification is a beneficial characteristic to instill in children, but is even that circumstantial? The runt of a puppy litter may not survive if it can't push its way to the mother's nipple. So, too, is survival for the child living in a difficult socioeconomic environment where it must compete with siblings who are less than caring and perhaps parents who are not as attentive to the child's needs as they should be. If the child fails to grab whatever opportunities present themselves for their immediate survival needs, survival is jeopardized. Delaying gratification under such circumstances might then be detrimental to the well-being of the child.

Long-term or short-term survivability often depends on circumstance. Learning discernment of circumstances then becomes the arbiter of decision-making, so that delaying gratification or partaking of instant gratification becomes a situational benefit directed to the survival needs of the individual under their unique circumstances. By any measure, it's a difficult lesson to learn and something researchers revisiting the famous Stanford "Marshmallow Test" of the 1970s concerning the benefits of delayed gratification discovered. In the original test, a marshmallow (or some other desirable treat) was placed in front of a child, and the child was told they could get a second treat if they just resisted the temptation for fifteen minutes. If they succumbed to the devilish pull of sugar, they only got the one. The researchers then followed up with the participants and found that those that could wait the fifteen minutes and delay gratification did much better on standardized tests, completed college at a far higher rate, and in general were more successful than those that could not hold out for the second marshmallow.[110]

The follow-up research, however, found that "there are more important—and frustratingly stubborn—forces at work that push or pull us from our greatest potential." And how what we first perceive as beneficial may not always be so under all circumstances. It's also important to realize that the young subjects in the original marshmallow test were from a narrow group. They all attended school on the Stanford campus and were children of professors or Stanford students, hardly a cross-section of society in general.[111]

Blame/Praise

Now that you are thoroughly uplifted, what about the ego's need for blame and praise regarding the belief in free will? We feel superior to others when we blame them for their misdeeds and superior again when we take credit for doing good in all fields of endeavor, often believing it was our hard work that accomplished the task, with little credit given to all the conditioning and support we have received. If there is no free will, blame and praise are meaningless—so too, for that matter, is a need for forgiveness.

Weak people revenge.
Strong people forgive.
Intelligent people ignore.
~ Albert Einstein

We may find ourselves fitting into one of these three categories, depending on the situation in which we find ourselves, rather than being identified as being one of them in all circumstances. But how can the last sentence (Intelligent people ignore) be true on a societal level? Einstein did not mean it on a societal level, but a personal one. On a societal level, wrongdoing is punished and good works are praised and rewarded. On a personal level, we have the possibility of being ahead or behind the developmental curve of society at large, just as those people who will not cheat simply because cheating is wrong. They need no law to keep them honest. This awareness is individually, not collectively, understood since it's been shown that a significant number of people will cheat given the chance to do so.

Uniqueness

It's obvious that laws are necessary for our present level of moral and ethical development. It's the only way we can hold large groups together for our common survival. Yet still, if there is some moral high ground, why do some inhabit it and others do not, and is that also part of our conditioning, since there is a moral readiness to do the right thing without a coercive element? Moral development has been studied extensively throughout history by theologians, philosophers, psychologists, and cultural theorists and we will look at some of those theories in the next section, but all things being equal?!?... No, wait! Full stop. Nothing in life is equal. From our physical development (as in the case of Michael Phelps) to every other element of our existence, we are as unique from one another as is one snowflake from another. Parents, education, birth order, environment, everything in our existence has conspired to make us incredibly special individuals with no one else on the planet having the same set of inputs as ourselves. The reality is that we are the only one of us and even if existence is all a movie that we are subjectively projecting from our minds, no matter determined or not, we are the only ones with our movie. We may have a consensus regarding something like morality, but within that consensus is an incremental ruler measuring the differences that make our view unique to our perception and life circumstances. We don't fully appreciate the person's capacities and limitations. The varied influences based on conditioning and genetic proclivities mitigate against the one-size-fits-all paradigms in societal institutions, yet based on our beliefs in things like free will, we remain simplistic in our application of cause and effect relationships for understanding the intricacies of human behavior. As complexity increases, so, too, must our societal mechanisms for approaching the human conditions that are inextricably bound up with the integration of the individual with society. These societal mechanisms are failing the individual's optimal growth potential and even though society may not be able to afford the luxury of an individually based learning model for education or law at present, we need to try to work toward that goal.

A Few Definitions

There is some confusion concerning the philosophical concepts of *fatalism* and *determinism*, which adds to the desire to believe in free will:

Fatalism is a doctrine that events are fixed in advance so that human beings are powerless to change them.[112] Since we don't know the future, but it is already fated, there's no use trying to do anything to change what may happen. Example: I may know that smoking cigarettes causes cancer but I shouldn't bother trying to stop smoking since if I'm meant to die from cancer there's nothing I can do about it, anyway.

Determinism is the theory that all events, including moral choices, are completely determined by previously existing causes.[113] We will, however, never know all the causes of everything, no matter the memory of our computers. Therefore, since we cannot "know" the future, some knowledge, even partial knowledge, allows us to make some educated guesses about cause and effect. Example: If I understand that smoking cigarettes can cause cancer, I can try and stop smoking because I also know my chances of dying from cancer will be diminished if I do so.

Compatibilism is the philosophical theory that tries to reconcile determinism and free will. It's the philosophical thesis that says free will is compatible with determinism, because free will is typically taken to be a necessary condition of moral responsibility. Compatibilism is sometimes expressed as the compatibility between moral responsibility and determinism.[114] This philosophy gives some moral, if not scientific, underpinning of why we need to believe in free will. And once again, society, at this stage of development, needs to believe in it to survive.

Fantasy: It seems, however, that Compatibilism is an artificial construct to satisfy our need to believe in free will. It's sort of like needing to believe in Santa Claus. As a child, the fantasy of the belief is preferable to reality: first, because the young child is more susceptible to fantasies and second, because we're getting some good stuff in exchange for belief. Therefore, as long as the fantasy can practically survive the onslaughts of external reality, the pleasure of the fantasy will go on. My grandson, for example, pretended to still believe in the tooth fairy even though he found out that it was his mom and dad who put a dollar or two under his pillow in exchange for a baby tooth. However, he also knew that if he stopped exhibiting the belief in the existence of the tooth fairy, the miraculous appearance of the money would stop. Better from his financial point of view to extend that belief as long as possible since he identified something good (money) with his belief; in short, the pleasure principle. The question at the time for me was, did my grandson have a free choice when he said he believed in the tooth fairy?

There is that period in childhood when we are developing our sense of what is real and not real, where belief includes make-believe playmates and monsters in our closets: friendly dinosaurs, Santa Claus, and the tooth fairy. Researchers have discovered that the fantasy-reality distinction in children is complex, but its study gives us some insight as to how beliefs are formed and how moral principles are developed over time.

Dating from the 1920s, studies have shown that children do not have a strong capacity to distinguish fantasy from reality until about the age of twelve. For example, they were often confused about whether dragons were real, and if someone dressed up as a ghost was an actual ghost.[115]

These findings were not universal but served to give some outer limits on when a sense of reality became much stronger compared to the child's relationship with fantasy. Much of children's fantasy beliefs depend on the right combination of age, evidence, and testimony, in which case children's belief in Santa Claus, the tooth fairy, and other fantastical beings, given all the strong parental and societal reinforcement, is very strong.[116] Let's also not forget that little feel-good release of dopamine in the child's brain after receiving the goodies, which puts that extra bit of icing on the cake of belief.

Conversely, children will also show a misplaced reliance on their own, limited knowledge and experience when they evaluate new information. For example, trying to explain to a three-year-old that the Earth is round does not comport with their experience and they are likely to disbelieve it. It was also true for four-year-olds who were told fantastical religious and non-religious stories; but when stories were said to be historically true, especially if told to the child by an authority figure like a parent or church leader, the default state for a child was to believe because disbelief takes extra cognitive work.

So, it was found that by age six, children who heard religious stories, for example, were more likely to claim the events and characters were real. In this case, skepticism decreased with age also, presumably, because children had cultural support and incorporated information from their religious communities for the stories they were told.[117] It should be said here that these behaviors are universal, not simply restricted to Western societies. The stories societies tell their children are part of the culture and are an integral part of the adaptive process by which individuals are integrated into the social order.

Belief

In the past ten to fifteen years, biology and neuroscience have opened the door to the mechanics of what happens to cells in our bodies and particularly in our brains as a result of conditioning and the thought processes we experience. We, in effect, become what we think due to the neuroplasticity of our brains. If we practice gratitude on a regular basis, for example, we become happier. If, on the other hand, we have a stream of negative thoughts, we may experience stress and depression. Take into account the ladder of inference along with these cellular changes formulating our belief systems and we have a perfect storm for good or ill.

Belief is a powerful motivator and there are reasons we cling to beliefs that at one point in time make sense but at another simply don't, yet which we continue to hold on to. We reason based on our emotional attachments to our beliefs and those emotional attachments are complex, involving biology, relationships, culture, and psychology. Letting go of negative beliefs can be painful, even when we know it's for our own good. Numerous self-help books and teachers are out there to help us with this process, but we also live in an age of endless distraction that encourages hanging on to negative thought patterns that make self-improvement more difficult. And does this have something to do with the fluidity of the concept of who we are?

No matter the stories told, fantastical or not, belief in them is the glue that holds the group together and without the buy-in of individuals, the society is threatened. For that reason, the personal narrative we tell ourselves is important. It gives us a way of communicating the things that we've perceived to others and allows us to develop survival strategies through our interpersonal relationships, which in turn allow us to predict the behavior of others.[118]

Education and indoctrination are part of society's methods for survival: One may be more heavily emphasized than the other, but both are present in every society, from hunter-gatherers to major nation-states. On the other hand, the bit of skepticism demonstrated by children in their early years may serve a larger purpose. Children are naturally curious; that curiosity allows for the "new" to enter society. Technology, novel ideas, and foreign cultural artifacts all effect changes in society. While perhaps not always for the better, societies inevitably change, be it through trade and communication or by war and domination. And since we don't have the luxury of choosing the times in which we live, our perception becomes the critical lens through which we judge our survivability in the milieu of our environment.

Esteem

People care a great deal more about appearance and reputation than about reality.[119] We can include Maslow's esteem needs here. For millions of years, our ancestors' survival depended on their ability to get small groups to include them, trust them, and think well of them.[120] Real or imagined, the need for both self-esteem and the respect of the community is a fundamental hierarchical need we desire to have fulfilled, whether these are well-deserved or sought only to inflate our egos, position, and prestige. Esteem is highly valued since it is important what others think about us. From our early childhood and the desire to please our parents to the adult world of professional recognition, working for that pat on the head becomes a major pursuit. Even research on self-esteem seems to support the idea that all of us unconsciously are constantly asking the question "How'm I doin'?" in just about every encounter we have.[121]

Often what we do becomes who we are, and our professions become a major part of our identities. Simply saying I'm a human being is not enough. It's necessary to gild the lily with the accouterments of accomplishment. Status depends on the caliber of the work we do. We feel a particular sense of gratification when we are admired by the people that we admire, and it's the approval of those who "know" that we seek primarily.

In the movie *Amadeus*, which was a dramatization of the life of Wolfgang Amadeus Mozart, the Habsburg court composer Antonio Salieri wrote a new work for the Vienna opera. After the opening night performance, which was attended by Emperor Joseph II and the royal court notables of Vienna, Salieri received a medal from the emperor honoring him as the greatest composer of his time. But rather than bask in the applause, Salieri looked around for Mozart, who was also in attendance. Salieri knew that despite his medal, Mozart was the greatest composer of the age, not him, and Salieri wanted his approval for his opera since Mozart's approval meant more to him than any honors that were given him by the emperor. This idea of merit is fundamental to our sense of being and the honors or acclamations bestowed by our peers are more meaningful than any others simply because they are given by those who know what goes into the work we do. Esteem, to be legitimate, must be merited, be it because we are the best hunter in the tribe or the best plumber in the town. We all care a lot about what other people think of us. The only people who don't are sociopaths.[122]

Reason

As discussed in Chapter 1, even animals cooperate and have genes for altruism, and those genes have been selected in the evolution of many creatures because of the advantage they confer for the continuing survival of the species.[123] After altruism on the hierarchy of brain development comes reason, the precursor for morality. "Reason" is designed to seek justification, not truth. In a new book titled *The Enigma of Reason*, cognitive scientists Hugo Mercier and Dan Sperber relate how "reason developed not to enable us to solve abstract, logical problems nor even help us draw conclusions from unfamiliar data; rather, it developed to resolve the problems posed by living in collaborative groups." Since humans are hyper-social the ability to cooperate depends on their capacity to get along in a group. Reason developed as an adaptation to make that happen. "Habits of mind that seem weird or goofy or just plain dumb from an 'intellectualist' point of view prove shrewd when seen from a social 'interactionist' perspective."[124]

We can imagine as a member of a hunter-gatherer group it would be smart to be accepting of the basic rules of the group, even if those rules appeared to be unjust or unfair since being ostracized from the group would most certainly mean death from any number of sources if we had to survive alone. We have to make choices but when it comes to our survival, are they really choices? The need to believe we are making a choice may be more important than the actual reality of a choice. We are held accountable, but how much of the process was coercion through manipulation? Contemporary politics seems also to bear this out at just about every turn, where often truth becomes subservient to group loyalty and that group ethos often has an element of superiority toward others. But, then, we feel good when we feel superior to others, when our tribe feels superior to other tribes, and when our nation feels superior to other nations. It comes back to our ego-selves and, by extension, to those groups with which we identify. Unfortunately, in-group-versus-out-group thinking warps the moral principles of liberals and conservatives alike.[125]

The Olympics are a good example of nationalism in full flower. Would we feel so good about them if we didn't win a basket full of medals every four years? Our national anthem gets to be played more than that of most other nations. There's great national pride that even the smaller nations feel when they just win a single medal or get close to winning just one. Thankfully, it's an internationally accepted benign form of war.

There is, of course, an upside. Competition challenges us to go beyond the limitations of the past. We improve everything from diet to new training methods in the attempt to shave a second or an inch off the records that have been broken before, and if we could get rid of war and just compete with sports and other benign areas of endeavor, wouldn't that be a wonderful thing?

Belief is an attitude that something is the case or that some proposition about the world is true. And just as in the child's ability to differentiate between fantasy and reality, we as humans have a hard time differentiating between belief and facts. The old adage, "you are entitled to your own opinion but not your own facts," is an example of the conflict between what we feel to be true and what is actually true based on factual evidence. We all fall victim to this problem—some more than others—but it's just so easy to slip into this thinking mode, particularly when we become emotional over a particular issue. Our moods become contextual, perfectly reasonable one moment and unreasonable the next. When we witness an election, for example, we see that in the words of historian Yuval Harari, "democracy is not based on human rationality, but human feeling."[126]

Judgment is an integral part of the individual and group psyche. Our ego-selves are hardwired to believe that "we" are more important than "them." And even though tribalism has become synonymous with xenophobia in contemporary society, it was and still is a necessary component of survival, including overcoming loneliness. Our human instincts are not designed for a solitary life, but for a life in a group. Our tribal associations are necessary for our survival since they meet our most fundamental needs.[127]

Loneliness is not just the absence of other people. It means not sharing anything of significance with anyone else.[128] We share gifts, cards, and favors. If we have little else, we share meals. That sharing connects us and makes us feel part of something larger than ourselves.

In order to end loneliness, we need to have a sense of "mutual aid and protection with at least one other person," and ideally with many others.[129] And that mutual aid and protection is basic survival. The larger the group, the more protected we feel. With this connection and conviction, it's only a small step to the reasons why we are superior, ultimately giving justification to why our survival is more important than theirs. It is "our" lives and our value system that ultimately count and looking out for number one is the underlying rationale for this attitude, usually supported by a healthy dose of "cognitive dissonance." The manifestation can be obvious or subtle, from the arrogant self-centered individual who never allows anyone else to speak in a conversation to the person who gloats over having a secret that no one else knows and feels a stronger sense of ego-self over others by cherishing this secret. Ego self-inflation always is the goal, often existing at a subconscious level.

Empathy

President Barack Obama famously claimed that the "empathy deficit" is a more pressing problem than the federal deficit. Is it an easy problem to solve? Shouldn't we just try and feel what it's like to walk in another person's shoes? Is it so difficult to feel another person's suffering? The answer is actually "yes."

There is no way, given another person's collective makeup, that we can actually feel what another person feels, save for very general characteristics that we can readily observe. We may, for example, be able to mirror their expression of pain and try to feel what it's like to be subject to the painful experience they may be going through, but that is only superficial. To know what it's like to be homeless and living on the street is something most of us will never understand. Nor is it likely we can understand what it's like to lose a child to a terminal disease or an accident unless that unfortunate circumstance has befallen us.

That's perhaps why the Dalai Lama suggests we cultivate compassion. Compassion does not judge or need to experience the same thing that another person experiences. It may be informed by empathy, but not bound by it to do good in the world. Compassion may not be difficult to exhibit in our group but, like empathy, extending it to strangers is more difficult. As Paul Bloom says in his book *Against Empathy*, "biases have causes that go deeper than empathy." It's natural that we should favor and care for our friends and family over strangers. Our group means more to us than people from other groups, since they are the ones who will look out for us, as we will reciprocate and look out for them. We don't know if we can trust different and possibly opposing groups to do the right thing. This is inevitable, given our evolutionary history, and any creature that didn't feel a special kinship toward his group would not survive from a Darwinian perspective.[130]

We can say, on the one hand, that the Dalai Lama shortcuts the route by which we can care about and help people by choosing compassion over empathy, but is there something else we need to learn through the process of empathizing with others that may take longer but is nonetheless valuable? There are two kinds of empathy, emotional and intellectual. Emotional empathy, which Bloom focuses on, is difficult. It means overcoming biases that are ingrained in us and extending that sense of self beyond our immediate circles. On the other hand, intellectual empathy is a simple rational thought process. "It's a deductive power that can be taught."[131] By teaching our children the basics—"What does this person think? How does this person feel? What is this person likely to do?"—it's easier for us to be compassionate since we start to understand that the other person has problems, too. We need not feel everything they feel to take a step in the right direction of intellectually identifying with them.[132]

Extending one's sense of self to others is essentially the mark of the mature individual. For some, it is only possible to encompass the family group and then the local tribe in this sense of self. We tend to call those folks xenophobic. The "other" is never very far away and the fear of the stranger is always close at hand. Others, however, manage to extend that sense of self to all of humanity. I suppose we tend to call those folks "saints." However, saints are not generally noted for longevity. But perhaps people like Daniel Lubetzky, founder and executive chair of Kind, LLC, exist just below that exalted level. He states: "For me, empathy is an existential question— it's about the survival of the human race. That is, it's imperative for us to overcome the challenges we face."[133] The challenges we face are no more pronounced than people experience in times of war. In his book *Ordinary Men* Christopher Browning addresses the responsibility German soldiers have for killing prisoners. He says,

I fear that we live in a world in which war and racism are ubiquitous, in which the powers of government mobilization and legitimization are powerful and increasing, in which a sense of personal responsibility is increasingly attenuated by specialization and bureaucratization, and in which the peer group exerts tremendous pressures on behavior and sets moral norms.[134]

Those moral norms are often in conflict with personal convictions and the concentric circles of empathy toward others increase or diminish with the ability to identify with those others or the lack thereof. How far can we go? And, as Bloom infers, will we suffer a loss by extending ourselves "too far?" Will we lose our community and, if so, what will that mean for us in both the short run and the long run?

We only need to look at those groups that have survived through the ages to see what aspects of group culture allowed for that survival. Marrying within the group was most important, as were traditions carried through time. Language, culture, the stories told, the heroes of the past, and religious beliefs that made them special, all play a role in group survival. Letting go of the need for that collective identity is no small feat. And even when we try to negotiate a compromise, there are always the purists within the group who will condemn all that would, in their minds, dilute the purity of the culture. Is it any wonder that after thousands of years it's still so difficult to love our neighbor, let alone our enemy? So why even bother trying? Isn't it better to live comfortably within our own society? Doesn't it feel good to be familiar with the rules of one's group, follow those rules, and be accepted rather than stretch the boundaries and be rejected by those who have most nurtured us and supported our efforts? That is, as long as those efforts supported the identity of the group.

Narcissism (Selfishness/Selflessness)

There is another direction by way in which we can view the issue of empathy or lack thereof—that is, by looking at it through the lens of narcissistic behavior. Mythology has long instructed us in the fundamental truths of human existence. The concept of self-love has a long history and one of the main characters in this theme was Narcissus. The Greek legend was of a beautiful lad who was prideful about his physical beauty.

He rejected the love of the nymph Echo, who then died of a broken heart. The god Nemesis punished Narcissus by making him fall in love with his own reflection in a lake. In admiring himself, he fell into the lake and drowned. The legend indicates that this kind of self-love is a curse and in its extreme form is self-destructive.[135] Psychologists since Freud have used this subject as a subheading under ego for explaining both a benign form of self-love and a negative form. Perhaps the psychologist and philosopher who has done one of the most comprehensive studies of the subject was Erich Fromm (1900–1980). Fromm called himself a humanist but further identified himself as a non-theistic mystic.[136] Some might find this a contradiction in terms, but Fromm's view of life was extremely broad, so he left no stone unturned in his search for truth and his interests were wide-ranging.

Fromm starts his explanation of narcissism with what he calls *primary narcissism*, that of the newborn child. It knows only itself and cares only for its immediate survival needs. Narcissism at this stage is a necessary energy source: without its singular focus the infant could not survive. Here narcissism provides a necessary biological function. When the child begins to recognize the mother as its source of sustenance and survival, it begins to extend its sense of self and identity with the mother gradually over time. And, as its awareness of its environment expands, and as we are beginning to understand through neuroscience, that sense of self begins to expand as well. The primary narcissism turns into *personal narcissism* and eventually as the child grows and starts to identify with family, etc., that sense of self expands to the larger group and develops into group narcissism. This is all part of a natural evolutionary process, which we also see in the animal world. It turns negative and sometimes into pathology when that sense of self cannot empathize with the "other" and becomes indifferent.[137] What is true of the individual is also true of the group. Narcissistic attachment does not allow us to see the other as we see ourselves. Those qualities most cherished are not what we have earned through our efforts but what we have (i.e., our looks, body, intelligence, wealth, things, etc.).

We also tend to seek out narcissistic leaders who mirror these qualities for us. In the negative form, the narcissistic leader who is convinced of his greatness and who has no doubts about it attracts those people who for those very reasons submit to him. They are superior because he is superior. The half-insane leader who gains power is most successful because he now can change circumstances to suit his reality, thereby confirming his greatness.

In societies in which the narcissistic leader cannot provide adequately for all its members, the practice of inducing narcissistic pride in the group will often suffice. This is common when pitting political, racial, or religious groups against one another. It's successful as long as the select group or groups are made to feel superior to other groups and, of course, it also helps to have scapegoats to blame for the problems of the country (Jews in Germany, Blacks in the South, Mexicans at the border, etc.). The narcissistic group identifies with what the leader tells them and, if it encounters criticism, "cognitive dissonance" gets in the way of any objective assessment, preventing clarity of thought. We can see this around the world as societies look for a "strong man" to lead them out of difficulty. Hitler, Stalin, Mussolini all took advantage of the troubles their countries faced at that time in history to offer simple solutions to complex problems. And although thankfully we don't have anyone at present rising to the level of Hitler, our age has its own host of goblins filling in some of the vacancies left by those who have gone before.

My country first (to the exclusion of the rest of the world) is part of the narcissistic populism that we have been witnessing around the world for the past decade. The tepid approach to climate change is perhaps foremost on the list. The Earth is caught in a Gordian knot of competition for national interests with only some of the more enlightened countries willing to take the plunge into actually doing something about the ecological disaster befalling our world. The saddest cut of all, however, is our inability to see the world that we are creating for our grandchildren. Selfishness does not just poison the bodies we inhabit, but the bodies they inhabit as well, and they have no say in the matter.

The cycle of narcissistic leaders usually lasts until they begin to make mistakes and their impotence, resulting from their lack of objective judgment, is revealed. Inevitably, through internal collapse, external force, or both, destruction follows.[138] But Fromm also believed the benign aspect of narcissism was a necessary evolutionary process that we needed to pass through to progress to a universal concept of love. It's a maturation process much like Maslow's Hierarchy. It's why when on an airplane we are instructed that in the case of an emergency, first put on your own oxygen mask before helping your child or anyone else put on theirs. In this case the airliner is the organism that must survive. The airline attendant is the brain telling us what to do to survive. Loving humanity is impossible without first loving ourselves, and those closest to us. From a biological point of view, it is self-preservation that is necessary before we can help anyone else and effectively contribute to the group. And not only from a psychological perspective but neurologically new research has shown that our brains prioritize ourselves over others, which makes sense from a survival perspective.[139] Fairness is okay as long as I get my fair share first. This, of course, makes extending that sense of self a process that we need to experience in stages—from the infant to the group, nation-state, and the world. It is a biological as well as a psychological and sociological process.

As our values develop, we see that narcissism conflicts with both reason and love. Just as some forms of love are possessive and insular, the more advanced forms are expansive. Fromm goes on to say that from the ethical spiritual point of view the essential teachings of all the great humanist religions can be summarized in one sentence: "It is the goal of man to overcome one's narcissism."[140] Overcoming one's narcissism is in effect transcending the ego-self.

Summary

When we reach the stage of development where we begin to focus on self-concepts, particularly those associated with what we have called the ego-self, and as our brain matures, we become cognizant of our desires and our need to fulfill those desires. We're beginning to expand beyond the basic physiological levels of Maslow's Hierarchy and start to focus on psychological needs and the development of our sense of the ego as the self that interacts with the world. We develop an identity through which we perceive the world and the view we have of ourselves. We learn techniques for getting what we want in order to satisfy some of the higher social needs that depend on a more sophisticated understanding of group dynamics and interpersonal relationships. We also begin to learn some of the limitations of our decision-making process and our concepts of free will. All of these behaviors continue to foster self-concepts that become gradually more expansive through social interaction and mutual dependency.

One of the problems in studying discrete disciplines (even though that is what's necessary to learn them in depth) is that the gray areas between them keep getting bigger. The understanding of nature versus nurture, for example, becomes ever more complex and as we have shown regarding the issue of selfishness versus selflessness, easy answers are harder to come by. The term narcissism has negative connotations, starting with the mythological story itself, but we can see from an evolutionary and biological perspective, it is necessary, at least for a time, so our brains prioritize our existence over others for survival. Secondarily, others begin to play a larger part in our existence, and without those others, we cannot grow. Short-term selfishness grows into long-term selflessness. Taking the long view, the process is not a psychological or biological anomaly, but rather a thing of evolutionary beauty.

I remember a saying but cannot place the origin, "There is no evil only lesser degrees of good." The closest I could find to this were similar sayings coming from the Baha'i faith. The act that appears negative in the short term often turns out to be positive in the long term. It's probably where the phrase "a necessary evil" comes from. The capacity for fair judgment usually depends on the proximity to harm of the person who is doing the judging. Hence the legal admonition, "not to take the law into your own hands," since judgment is difficult enough even when we believe we know all the facts of a given incident.

Neuroscience is beginning to explain the origins of pathologies resulting from deficiencies or excesses in the chemistry and neural activity of the brain. It's both confirming and contradicting long-held psychological beliefs that have influenced public opinion for many years, both for good or ill. That reality prompts this story: Some years ago, I was watching a TV interview with country and western singer Willie Nelson on the occasion of his eightieth or eighty-first birthday, and the interviewer asked, "Willie, what good advice would you give to your younger nineteen-year-old self?" Willie, without hesitation said, "Shut up." We are all eager to inform or brag to others about our discoveries, including this writer. But perhaps we need to listen a bit more to the sage advice of that country singer and take a little more time before we make our pronouncements.

Chapter 3

Making Connections

At all costs I, or what I perceive as "me" must survive. We have seen that it may not be the physical aspects of my being, although at one level of evolution that certainly would be preferable. It could be in the form of my offspring or the group to which I belong. But we've gone from non-sentience to this narcissistic ego-centered self to the ability to expand that sense of "I am" to family and tribal association and, if more evolved, to nation and possibly world identity. But why? What's the point? Is there, indeed, a point? It has been our hope that in using Maslow's (Expanded) Hierarchy of needs that a directionality in evolution would become evident. This final chapter explores the belief that there is, in fact, directionality beyond chaos. And if there is directionality, where is it going? In this last section we would like to connect the physical to the metaphysical and possibly see if it makes any sense.

Moral Development

Well, transcending the ego-self is easier said than done, Dr. Fromm. But perhaps evolution helps us along this road in a baby step-like fashion, one small step at a time adding incrementally to this seeming monumental goal.

Moral development seems to be one of the most important steps along the way. We discussed a bit in the first chapter about how morality began to develop in the animal world through reciprocity, altruism, kin relationships, cooperation, and even friendships. In the human world, we actually discuss moral principles and schools of ethics. We can view morality through a cognitive lens not privy to our animal friends. And now we have science that can help us out with things like brain imaging to track our neurological map. We can then test the transmission of dopamine, which is what triggers our pleasure centers and at the same time causes us to get bored when our expectations are not met. We understand that testosterone increases aggression and impulsive behavior, that oxytocin facilitates trust and bonding, and adrenaline stimulates our little gray cells vibrating us into action. Our philosopher forebears would be green with envy to have the information that is at our fingertips today. But when we get down to talking about the subject of moral judgment, it's not a purely cerebral affair in which we weigh concerns about harms, rights, and justice. Rather, the process becomes more automatic or, from the neuroscientist point of view, rests with the amygdala.[141] And when we get to some things like relationships or choosing leaders, it's mostly about feeling. Having a check sheet with tabulation boxes doesn't always help.

Back to Darwin, we see that he was aware of the importance of emotions in his book *On the Origin of Species*.[142] He believed that humans shared emotional and cognitive capacities with other animals, including tool use, language, aesthetic sensitivity, even religions and morality, if only in their rudimentary form.

There can be no doubt that a tribe, which included many members with a high degree of the spirit of patriotism, fidelity, obedience, and courage, and were always ready to aid one another and to sacrifice themselves for the common good, would likely be victorious over most other tribes. This would be natural selection.[143]

Emotions

There's no getting around it, no matter the view we have of ourselves as rational beings, our emotions play a major role in how we make decisions. Our emotional brain has been developed for at least 200 million years. Our "rational" neocortex, only about 1.8 million years, which makes it a relative latecomer in the area of brain development. And the development of language and symbol systems is even younger. So, as a collection of coping tools our "emotions" have been around for a lot longer than "rational cognition." Therefore, when it comes to the "go to" area of the brain as a first responder, it's usually the amygdala that answers that call first. And that may be where the phrase "shoot first, ask questions later" comes from.[144] But, isn't this line of reasoning what humans do? We tend to focus on the newest whiz-bang thing to come along and think that it's the end-all-be-all. Even if that new thing happens to be 1.8 million years old. We recognize that we've developed a prefrontal cortex and now can be deliberative, yet we still fall back on feelings to make so many decisions. Evolution has provided us with additive brain capacity. That doesn't mean those regions that developed earlier are no longer vitally important and no longer hold surprises for our understanding. We are still in our infancy as far as understanding all the uses of each region of the brain and how they interact with one another.

So, was Descartes right when he said "I think therefore I am"? Or should it be "I feel therefore I am"? But, think or feel, the one thing we cannot deny is our own existence. And although we may not necessarily know if animals have a sense of ego, we do know that many have a sense of self (that may or may not be the same thing). In the human world, we cannot divorce ego development from moral development, since a person's sense of morality is part and parcel of the ego-self. And just as we can study different parts of the body, we can study different aspects of the ego.

Ideas about moral development have existed for centuries from theologians and philosophers like Confucius and Aristotle to developmental theorists like Jean Piaget and Lawrence Kohlberg. Psychologists, starting with Freud, have put their opinions to work on the subject, and psychology, in general, has dominated the study of moral development for many decades. How moral decisions are made is complex and extends over a lifetime, with stages of development tied to age and experiences. When we add in the neurological and bio-evolutionary factors, it becomes obvious just how complex the understanding of the whole process is. New research shows that there may even be genetic factors that contribute to moral decisions within families. They are not necessarily deterministic, absent conditioning experiences, but do give a higher degree of potentiality than exists with unrelated individuals.[145]

Moral Theories

We're going to go over two of the more recent moral development theories. They are given as examples and are not intended to be comprehensive, particularly since both point to the concept of our ego-self. Lawrence Kohlberg, who built on the work of Freud and Piaget, developed the first. He believed there were six stages of moral development, hierarchical in the sense that each stage was more adequate to respond to the increasing moral complexity than the previous. The young child, for example, does not need the same level of complexity in dealing with moral decisions as the adolescent. To some degree, Kohlberg's stages also correspond to brain development, with the amygdala developing before the prefrontal cortex and the corresponding behavior outcomes dependent on the degree of brain development.

Kohlberg's Six Stages of Moral Development

Kohlberg's theory of moral development defined three levels: preconventional, conventional, and postconventional. Each level has two distinct stages:

Preconventional Morality:

> Stage 1 (ages two to six): Obedience and punishment. The child is motivated to avoid punishment and has little or no

independent moral reasoning.

Stage 2 (ages five to nine): Individualism and exchange. Individuals are focused on fulfilling their own self-interests while acknowledging that different people have different views.

Conventional Morality:

Stage 3 (ages seven to twelve): Maintaining interpersonal relationships. At this stage, individuals emphasize the importance of being kind to other people, engaging in "good" behavior and showing concern for others. This stage includes a strong emphasis on gaining approval.

Stage 4 (ages ten to fifteen): Law and order. The individual is determined to obey the rules, focusing on the value that the law adds to human life. A person at this stage might argue that breaking the law is wrong because the law is designed to protect people. Stage 4 individuals focus on maintaining the social order and upholding cultural norms.

Postconventional Morality:

Stage 5: Social contract. People at this stage of development focus on doing what is best for society as a whole and respecting individual rights. Civil disobedience would be endorsed by people in both stages of postconventional morality.

Stage 6: Universal principles. At this stage, individuals are focused on upholding principles of universal justice, fairness, and ethics. They believe in the democratic process but also endorse disobeying unjust laws.[146]

A Quick Summary of Kohlberg's Six Stages

The first level of moral thinking is generally found at the elementary school level. In the first stage of this level, people behave according to socially acceptable norms because they are told to do so by some authority figure (e.g., parent or teacher). This obedience is compelled by the threat or application of punishment. The second stage of this level is characterized by a view that the right behavior means acting in one's own best interests.

The second level of moral thinking is that generally found in society, hence the name "conventional." The first stage of this level (stage 3) is characterized by an attitude that seeks to do what will gain the approval of others. The second stage is one oriented to abiding by the law and responding to the obligations of duty.

The third level of moral thinking is one that Kohlberg felt is not reached by the majority of adults (similar to Maslow's "Self-Actualization" level). Its first stage (stage 5) is an understanding of social mutuality and a genuine interest in the welfare of others. The last stage (stage 6) is based on respect for universal principles and the demands of individual conscience. While Kohlberg always believed in the existence of stage 6 and had some nominees for it, he could never get enough subjects to define it, much less observe their longitudinal movement to it.

Kohlberg believed that individuals could only progress through these stages one at a time. That is, they could not "jump" stages. They could not, for example, move from an orientation of selfishness to the law-and-order stage without passing through the good person stage. They could only come to a comprehension of a moral rationale one stage above their own. Thus, according to Kohlberg, it was important to present them with moral dilemmas for discussion, which would help them to see the reasonableness of a "higher stage" morality and encourage their development in that direction.[147]

Loevinger's Ego Development Theory (EDT)

The second moral development theory we're looking at was originally developed by Jane Loevinger (1918–2008) who was an assistant to the famous behavioral psychologist Erik Erickson in graduate school. It is titled *Ego Development Theory* (EDT) and is the one that is most important for this book since it is inclusive of those ideas that have gone before and inextricably ties moral development to the ego. In Loevinger's model the ego is described "as a process, rather than a thing." It's a "lens" or a "frame of reference" we use to view and interpret our world. Each stage of development shows how we organize and understand our experiences over our lifetimes. We build the new stage and integrate it with the previous one as we develop and mature.[148] (As in Kohlberg's model, no one can skip a stage.)

As the adult ego develops, Loevinger believed a sense of self-awareness in which one becomes aware of discrepancies between conventions and one's behavior emerges. Some people reach plateaus and don't continue. Others continue and move on to further ego integration and differentiation.[149] Loevinger believed that there were nine stages and that most adults do not reach the final stages. The stages include:

1. **Presocial (infancy):** The baby, which is at the mercy of the world around it (and its own needs), really has no ego to speak of until it begins to differentiate itself from its caregivers and the demands of the outer environment. **Impulsive:** The young child is driven by its emotions, including sexual and aggressive drives, and interprets caregiver responses in black and white terms as either being "nice to me" or "mean to me." The world is "good" if it meets her needs and "bad" if it doesn't. The child's focus is on present events rather than being caught up in the past or future.

2. **Self-protective:** The child at this stage begins to develop

some rudimentary self-control. His ideal is of a morally rigid and unchanging world of rules and norms that specify how he is to act. He's caught up in perceiving the world in terms of punishments and rewards, but also incorporates the need "not to get caught." **Conformist:** The child now becomes more aware of society and the need to belong to a group with its own biases and stereotypes (such as the gender groups of "boys" or "girls"). Good behavior is what is sanctioned by one's group, and others outside the group are treated with suspicion. An important element in terms of cohesion to the group is a sense of trust in one's fellow members.

3. **Self-aware:** Loevinger believed that this stage represents the model for most adult behavior, with few going beyond this stage before age twenty-five. Here we see the beginnings of self-criticism and the ability to envision multiple possibilities in life events. There's an increasing awareness of the difference between the "real me" and the "expected me" although the ego is still partly influenced by conformist pressures.

4. **Conscientious:** Individuals in this stage have internalized the rules of society, but they also acknowledge the existence of exceptions and special contingencies. The ego feels guilt for hurting others rather than feeling remorse at breaking the rules. The person at this stage sees life in terms of the choices that she makes and the responsibility she takes for her own actions. Views of other people are more complex at this stage and include their inner motives as well as their outer actions.

5. **Individualistic:** This stage includes respect for individuality in oneself and a tolerance toward the individual differences in others. The person at this stage is more sensitive to the complexities of inner experience

and the conflict between subjective reality and outward appearances.

6. **Autonomous**: Achieving a sense of self-fulfillment becomes more important than outer achievement at this stage. There is greater self-acceptance and deeper respect for the autonomy of others. There's a greater capacity to embrace the polarities of life, to discern complexity in individual situations and to assess multiple facets in moral decisions.

7. **Integrated**: This stage is similar to Maslow's concept of "self-actualization." The ego shows inner wisdom, deep empathy for others, and a high degree of self-acceptance. This is the stage of a fully formed and mature ego that cherishes individuality in self and others. Loevinger says that very few people make it to this stage.[150]

Picking up on Loevinger's ego development theory was Susan Cook-Greuter who refined EDT over the past forty years and expanded on what she believes makes EDT unique in the field of developmental psychology. She concludes that EDT addresses the whole person and portrays the growth of the individual integrated with the world around them. There is no separate interior development outside the context of environment. They are interrelated. She believes that the basic human drive for differentiation and integration could be observed, both overall and from stage to stage. While at the same time, the individual is striving to make sense of reality and add meaning to life.[151]

I emphasize this overall connectedness here because this theory also points out that no aspect of life exists purely on its own. The phrase "no man is an island" is a truism for all life. The seesaw back and forth between separateness and connectedness is the constant play of duality sitting ever in the lap of ego. Susan Cook-Greuter was also aware of the possibility of even more advanced stages of ego-development that have yet to be explored, just as Maslow believed there were other realms beyond Self-actualization.

In the mid-1960s, psychologists first postulated that human beings individuate by continuously renegotiating the balance between differentiation and integration, between the individual and the group. The group may be represented by any social unit—the family, tribe, nation—or by an ideology; extend it far enough and it could be represented by the universe. This dual need can be expressed by other names as well: separation and participation, independence and connection, or individualism and communalism. This is also similar to Fromm's sense of individual and group narcissism, the identification with the self and with the group, but gradually shedding all selfish aspects of narcissistic self-centeredness.[152]

Individual and the Group

The struggle is to constantly find the balance between individualism and communalism. It is always tenuous. If the balance is too far in the direction of self-expression, the group will suffer from a lack of energy related to group purpose. The individual's focus will not be sufficiently on the group but on oneself. Conversely, if the individual's energy is forced too far in the direction of the group or group unity, the individual will be suppressed and not achieve their highest potential, which will ultimately weaken the group since by minimizing the flourishing of the individual, the group potential is eventually diminished. Different cultures prioritize one aspect or the other, with the right balance often difficult to attain since the evolution of the culture is often predicated on one or the other paradigms.

Americans are generally on the side of individualism as being a primary attribute of American culture. The idealized image of the self-sufficient cowboy is an example. That perception of the "rugged individualist," someone who can pull themselves up by their bootstraps, is to be respected. Even regarding the concept of altruism, Americans conditioned by this individualist ethos have developed somewhat of a jaundiced eye regarding the true need of the poor, ascribing a certain amount of blame to the victims as being somehow not trying hard enough to alleviate their own condition. We have even developed a term for our beneficence toward the poor, "skeptical altruism." In other words, we believe in both giving to the poor while blaming them for their circumstances. Unfortunately, this attitude prevents us from systemically addressing the problems of poverty.[153]

The Japanese and Chinese on the other hand are generally more group identity-oriented, with the belief that too much emphasis placed on the individual leads to arrogance and selfishness. "If the nail stands up, hammer it down" becomes a cultural maxim. The opposing political systems of capitalism and communism tend to also exemplify those two realities, and although we can see refinements of those systems in some national governments, the political landscape still appears to vie between these extremes.

Beyond the Pull of Opposites

Societal and political proclivities may favor one approach or the other regarding the individual and the group, but our brains seem to need both. Recognizing that need is a starting point. It's hard to imagine a person reaching their full potential without having a substantial amount of solitude or alone time. It may not be the same thing as the emphasis on rugged individualism, but I would suggest that there is a connection. Focus on the self, even that ego-self we've been talking about, drives us to satisfy our desires. Without that drive, accomplishing anything becomes difficult and climbing Maslow's Hierarchy requires desire. And the skill set necessary to reach the upper levels of Maslow's Hierarchy can only be attained by including a certain amount of solitude in one's life.

In today's world of social media and a sense of constantly

being in touch, trying to find a time and place to be alone becomes increasingly more difficult. We are constantly checking in with someone or a group of people through social media. The workplace invades our "off-time" like never before and the expectation that we are available whenever someone wants to connect with us has become the norm for many people. Psychologists try to remind us of the necessity for a certain amount of solitude and the advantages taking the time to be alone has for us, but for many it's an uphill battle. Just to give a brief list of advantages, here are six science-based reasons why solitude is good for us:

1. Solitude allows a reboot of our brains and an opportunity to unwind.
2. Solitude helps improve concentration and increase productivity.
3. Solitude gives us an opportunity to discover ourselves and find our voice.
4. Solitude provides time for us to think deeply.
5. Solitude helps us work through problems more effectively.
6. Solitude can enhance the quality of our relationships with others.[154]

And, of course, creativity and self-reflection are all but impossible without a certain amount of alone time. Yuval Harari, historian, major contemporary thinker, and author of *New York Times* bestsellers *Homo Dias, Sapiens* and *20 Lessons for the 21st Century,* said that without his two hours of meditation a day and his thirty- to sixty-day silent retreats each year, he could not have written the books he has.[155]

It would seem, given any reasonable definition of "rugged individualist," Yuval Harari would certainly qualify, even without owning a horse. Yet, if anyone reads any of his books, they will see that his understanding of the connectedness of people and the mechanisms by which that connectedness occurs are extremely insightful.

Harari may be a bit on the extreme end of needing alone time in the hustle and bustle of our modern age, but all we need to do is google "solitude" or the benefits thereof and we will come across numerous studies and self-help sites that give a world of information on the subject. Add "meditation" to the search and you'll find an entire library on the benefits of the practice and how to do it, starting with just a few minutes a day.

The recognition of individuation and separateness is part of our biological and psychological drive. Ignoring them simply dooms the longevity of any society, something the Soviet Union discovered too late. At the same time, the need for relationships and community is also part of our human evolutionary makeup. Capitalism, taken to the extreme, risks the same destructive future. Recognizing the need to balance individuation with the need for community is often a difficult juggling act, but one critically necessary if a society is to survive.

Relationships

Internationally known psychologist Dan Goleman, writer of *Emotional Intelligence* and *Social Intelligence*, describes what he calls a "neural duet" which helps the brain integrate our ongoing interactions and attachment to others necessary for emotional balance and regulation.[156]

Along those same lines, philosopher and psychologist Louis Cozolino writes in his book *The Neurobiology of Relationships* "the brain depends on interactions with others for its survival." He gives the example that "if we isolate one neuron in a Petri dish, it won't survive very long; it needs the connections with other neurons to survive. The same is true if we, in effect, isolate our brains by hiding out from interdependent connections."[157]

No one ever said this process was easy, but luckily for us

the neural plasticity of the brain allows for change even when our conditioning mitigates against it. But the willingness to change our behavior has to be present to get to a state of healthy interdependence. Patterns developed from childhood are tough to reorganize, since they've created neural pathways that are stubborn to reroute, with old habits simply continuing to be destructive in our lives. The likelihood of making negative choices in relationships, and so on, is simply so easy to fall back into. Our conditioning needs to be reconditioned. The good news is that our brain's plasticity to grow new pathways and new neurons allows for the rewiring of our brain throughout our life, barring any unforeseen disease that would affect the brain.[158] We know that things like mindfulness practice works. It's not about religion or joining a group, but if we want to make changes in our life that require attitudinal adjustment, being a mental couch potato makes the process difficult. The effort also has nothing to do with intellectual giftedness: In fact, being very bright often allows for more complex rationalizations for reasons why we shouldn't make any changes.

All politics are local. Local down to the individual relationship level. What exists relationally in the macrocosm exists in the microcosm, society as a whole being an expansion of interpersonal relationships. Just as a bad interpersonal relationship can be destructive to personal growth, so too can a group have the same negative or positive influence on an individual. As we've said before, we can't survive for long alone, but that group need may also be destructive, and we need to know when it's time to leave or change groups.

The pressure to conform may be subtle or extreme: Let's not forget Galileo and the Church. But that's on the grand historical scale. What about our group of friends or relatives? Our comfort zone is also part of our survival zone. We depend on friends to be supportive and to be there for us when we have needs to be met. So when do the edges of relationships get frayed to the point of breaking? When are they beyond recovery? So many self-help books say pretty much the same thing: "What are your basic beliefs?" Politics, love, philosophy, or religion often come down to those basics of life that we have to ask about when it comes to relationships and their survivability. Do we have enough compatibility in those areas to make it work? A person or a group can help us soar or suffocate. Staying or leaving becomes a major life decision. And, of course, the book suppliers are full of self-help books giving plenty of advice for exactly what to do, along with a long line of internet sources anxious to be at your service.

Groups that, on the one hand, do a lot of good also may have a terminal point for an individual when they begin to hold him or her back. We may be inspired to grow and move progressively forward, but then be held back by cultural, institutional, or intellectual rigidity that begins to stunt any future growth. Knowing when to leave is difficult. The same thing that makes us feel good often restrains us: friendships, loyalties, culture, family ties, possibly finances, and position. The dilemma is not so different than knowing when to leave an interpersonal relationship.[159]

We cannot always be content moving at the pace of the group. Sometimes we must break away to grow. And we must understand that it's not always possible to change a group from within. History is full of failed attempts to do so, therefore know your own capacity. Political systems or interpersonal relationships all have non-zero or zero-sum potential. Learning techniques for growth within a group are helpful, but sometimes nothing works but leaving. We must "survive" and simply existing is not surviving. We are in a constant state of growing or dying. Change is the only thing we can count on.

The philosopher Heraclitus (530–470 BC) is a good starting point for anyone concerned with a change in life. Heraclitus noted: "Everything is constantly shifting, changing, and becoming something other than what it was before." Heraclitus concluded that nature is change. Like a river, nature flows ever onwards. Even the nature of the flow changes. The fact that we can never step into the same river twice was his idea, and we might say he was the first guy who prompted to "go with the flow" and enjoy the ride, as wild as it may be.[160]

Looking at Loevinger's Ego Development Theory, we can see that we are in a constant state of change. It might be rapid or glacial depending on our circumstances, but change is always our companion, so why not make the most of it?

Human development in many ways moves through different stages of making sense of reality.[161] But no matter the path we follow, when all is said and done, we want to be happy. Survival is the given. Self-preservation is the ultimate motivator and although philosophers and teachers of all persuasions offer us theories and outlines for growth, experience is the teacher that is the proof of the pudding.

Peak Experiences

Peak experiences are often described as altered states of consciousness. They are characterized by euphoria, most often achieved by self-actualized individuals but not restricted to them. Sometimes in the course of our lives we need to be knocked over (physically or metaphorically) to "get it." Like a physical shock shaking us out of a mental stupor, a peak experience can wake us up to realities of which we were totally unaware. The "it" is what becomes fascinating. Since the event was out of the realm of our normal experience, we are automatically intrigued by it and become interested in finding out more about the experience. The experience is more than just the little light bulb going off in our heads when we wake up in the morning with the answer to a problem we have been working on or those occasional "a-ha" moments that impress us. No, it usually comes with more of a bang, at least in the initial stages. People have had life-changing psychedelic experiences that opened them up to understandings previously blocked by mountains of conditioned taboos. Other peak moments may be brought on by intense meditative experiences, athletics, artistic events, or encounters with nature that left us full of wonder. The point is that in one way, shape, or form, these moments were life changing.

Flow

Heraclitus gave us an original idea of flow in nature and the suggestion of going with it.

Mihaly Csikszentmihalyi is a Hungarian-American psychologist. He recognized and named the psychological concept of flow, which is a highly focused mental state conducive to productivity. The sense of "flow" as explained by Csikszentmihalyi is one aspect of those higher states that some call peak experiences. Here is what an American composer he was interviewing said when the composer recounted an experience composing music:

> You are in an ecstatic state to such a point that you feel as though you almost don't exist. I have experienced this time and again. My hand seems devoid of myself, and I have nothing to do with what is happening. I just sit there watching it in a state of awe and wonderment. And [the music] just flows out of itself.

The state of ecstasy, by definition, is not an ordinary state of consciousness. It has some very different meanings, but in the original from the Greek *ekstasis* means, "to be or stand outside oneself."[162]

In this composer's state, he seemed to be an observer watching himself, experiencing this altered state of mind. When our composer starts the creative process, something happens and he enters a different state of reality. It also should be mentioned here that this flow state does not happen every time he or any other person sits down to write music or do any other creative undertaking. That's where the phrase "he was visited by the muse" comes into play. But, when it does happen, the experience may be extremely powerful, to the point where the composer said that the experience was so intense "that you feel as though you almost don't exist."

Csikszentmihalyi goes on to explain what neuroscience says about our capacities in this area, which may at least explain some of the mechanical workings that are going on. It appears that our nervous system is incapable of processing more than 110 bits of information per second. It's why we have a very difficult time understanding more than two people talking to us at the same time. To hear and process what one person is saying takes 60 bits per second. When we are thoroughly engaged in creating a new piece of work like the composer above, we don't have enough attention left to monitor how we are feeling or what's going on at home, etc. In his case, he didn't even feel hungry or tired. Everything, including his mind and body, felt temporarily suspended.[163] Research has shown that many people have experienced this feeling of flow or even ecstasy in many fields of endeavor, and not just in the artistic fields. Mathematicians, athletes, and many others have had this experience. There are many levels of this kind of experience, but they are usually marked by doing things we enjoy at a very high level and a sense of passion with the involvement. Anxiety, on the other hand, is a sure killer of the flow state. Perhaps because anxiety is so linked to fear.

Some of the most forward-looking companies have now become aware of the concept of "flow" in the workplace environment. When Masaru Ibuka was starting Sony Corporation, he had neither money nor any particular product, but he had an idea. Masaru wanted to establish a workplace where engineers can feel the joy of technological innovation, be aware of their mission in society, and work to their heart's content. This is an example of how "flow" is introduced in the workplace. Managers and employers can't make it happen, but they can facilitate the atmosphere to make it more conducive to occur.

Now back to the composer for a minute. When he said, "he felt almost as if he didn't exist," who was it that didn't exist and who then was the observer watching his body go through the motions? If those questions are valid because he did not have a sense of his body acting, who was composing the music? Was it a visiting muse? Well, the medical profession attempts to give some answers for this phenomenon in a definition of depersonalization-derealization disorder which "occurs when we persistently or repeatedly have the feeling that we're observing ourself from outside our body or we have a sense that things around us aren't real or both." The causes are not well understood. Some people appear to be more susceptible than others and high levels of stress may also be involved. Many people have a passing experience of depersonalization or derealization, but they are rare and have no serious side effects. The cure seems to be psychotherapy and sometimes medication is also used.[164]

But let's not jump to a mental illness for our composer just yet. Maybe something else is going on. Before our composer could get to the point of entering the flow state, he had to let go of his need to control everything. The preparation and skill-building necessary came long before, when he had to put in many years of concentrated practice at his craft. The facility needed to simply write the notes down on paper requires many hours of dedicated work just to learn the theoretical craft of music, and just like writing a letter, for some it is a laborious task, and for those with great facility in both language and grammar, it comes as second nature. That trust in our ability is a prerequisite for the flow state to exist. There are also other pre-requisites: a feeling of body-mind unity on the task; concentration on the task at hand; a sense of control and no fear of failure; a fluid sense of time; loss of self-consciousness; and enjoying the task for its own sake.[165] When it embodies the above qualities any work can become an art.

Our ego has a difficult time with these last two prerequisites for the flow state above. It's hard to let go of our belief in being the doer. It's also difficult to simply do things for their intrinsic value. We want the reward and appreciation for the work we do. We might even say that some of the upper levels of Maslow's Hierarchy of Needs are dependent, to a large extent, on this realization. "Self-esteem" requires confidence in one's worth and abilities; "Need for Aesthetics," the flow state itself is a space of beauty; "Self-actualization," is the complete realization of one's potential and the full development of one's abilities and appreciation for life. According to Maslow, not everyone reaches this "Self-actualized" state of being, just as not everyone achieves the flow state, at least not for extended periods. But even glimpses of this reality can entice us to strive for more of these experiences. And, like a drug, flow can be addictive, and the fact that we cannot attain it at will enhances its value. But why do we want to experience it? Perhaps like good food, once we've had it, returning to poor food can never again satisfy our taste. So, if the optimal living condition is living in a state of flow, does it become one more desire to be satisfied?

Characteristics of the Flow State:

1. Action and awareness merge
2. Sense of self vanishes
3. All aspects of performance heighten
4. Sense of time distorts[166]

Csikszentmihalyi defines the flow state as: "A state of complete immersion in an activity." He describes the mental state of flow as "being completely involved in an activity for its own sake. The ego falls away."

Well, here we are again, back to the ego. To achieve our optimum performance level the ego needs to "fall away" or be transformed. Different psychological approaches use different terminology. For some philosophies the ego must be transcended, for others it must be transformed. It may simply be a matter of semantics. Even the ancient practices of Buddhism and Advaita Vedanta have similar but different explanations of the "ego-self." In Buddhism, the goal is "no-self" or the extinguishment of the sense of self. In Advaita, it is a transformation of the ego-self to an enlightened state of being, as identification of being one with all existence or what is called "non-duality" or "oneness." Duality is what we might call our ordinary consciousness: a sense of separateness with existence. Perhaps even in Christianity there is that explanation of a state of oneness when Christ said, "I and my father are one." Two thousand years ago the statement screamed "blasphemy" to many in the Jewish community. And even today in some countries bridled with the orthodoxy of literal belief, it has the same ring. But as philosophy and science march forward, the semantic similitude begins to break down and the idea of becoming one with existence loses some of the fire and brimstone of an earlier age. The duality of the I-Thou relationship with God becomes more open to interpretation since the idea of a divine source is now viewed more as a concept and is less boxed in by narrow perception and limited imaginations. Take a step back from our attachment to *-isms* and there is no real reason, for example, that a materialistic view of existence cannot coexist comfortably with non-duality. There is no prerequisite for a divine aspect to be part of the understanding. What is necessary, however, is an admission that what we don't know concerning first causes is far greater than what we do know. For example, is there any consensus on what happened before the Big Bang?

The Doer

It is difficult to let go of the sense of doership. After all, if I accomplish something why shouldn't I claim I did it? The ego-self is constantly claiming credit. There is the ego need to claim credit as the doer. Why not? It makes us feel good to be given credit for our accomplishments. Why have a sense of false modesty or minimize what we have done? If I do something noteworthy, don't I deserve the credit? Is there no such thing as a "healthy ego"? Psychology is full of articles and studies concerning developing healthy ego strengths and the benefits of having a healthy ego. A healthy ego serves the purpose of helping us remain grounded amid the chaos of the world.[167]

When we look at Maslow's recognition of self-actualization as being the highest goal (at least in his original hierarchy), that "healthy" ego-self is certainly part of that attainment. But contrast this need for credit or blame, for that matter, with the state of "flow," where that sense of doership does not exist. Things are done, but there is no doer. One can argue, of course, that there is a doer. After all, somebody climbed the mountain or played the concerto or did the work. How can there not be a doer? The answer from the non-dualist point of view is yes, the act was done but identification with the act is what causes the separateness of the ego-self. That is the illusion of duality. The ego-self takes credit for the act, thereby separating itself from the oneness of existence when in reality it is only one aspect of existence. Existence itself has done it. So just as the hand of a body cannot take the credit for lifting a glass separate from the interconnectedness of the brain and all the neural networks in the body making it happen, so too can we not take credit for what we claim to do separate from the rest of our interconnected existence that made it possible. Even our attitudes to do something on our own may have been conditioned by circumstances of which we are completely unaware. A lack of support, for example, can motivate some individuals to accomplish a great deal just to prove to the naysayers they could do it. Then it just becomes another attachment to the ego-self's sense of doership.

From the Advaita Vedanta or non-dualist point of view, it is all real, depending on the perspective taken. In other words, if we are in a dream, the dream is real from the perspective of the dreamer. When we wake up, we realize we were dreaming. The ego-self is the dreamer believing it is the doer. When we wake up and realize we are one with all of existence we no longer see ourselves as the dreamer or the doer but simply part of the doing.

We are the puppet and the puppet master. We dance to the tune and we write the tune and play the music at the same time. We exist in the state of "I Am." There is no "other" for comparison. There is no separateness, save the illusion we have created in the dream we are dreaming. At that point of conscious awareness, true free will exists. We are one with infinite reality: There is no separate will and we are truly free.

How does one accomplish this? The same way the musician gets to Carnegie Hall—practice.

But what kind of practice?

Ways of Knowing

How can we know any of this to be true? It sounds like a lot of New Age woo-woo. Conversely, it also may sound like a lot of ancient beliefs that have been around forever. If this makes us question more or just put it down as gibberish, we have lots of company on either side of the equation. The questioning itself has questions though. The questions have to do with "ways of knowing" or the philosophical discipline of the "theory of knowledge" or "epistemology." That's the branch of philosophy that deals with the question of how we know what we know (or believe we know). And, beyond that, we must look at those different ways of knowing. It's a massive subject by itself, so we cannot attempt to address all the questions, but merely look at some of the broad ideas.

In recent years there has been an expansion of the premises as to how we know what we know or the different ways of knowing. This is where our personal biases enter the picture. Some of the ways of knowing in the following list will be held up or put down, based on our own particular biases and backgrounds. This doesn't mean that when applied to different areas of study, one way of knowing may not be more efficacious than another, only that when given our different personalities, experiences, and conditioning, we may be prone to prefer one way of knowing over another and thereby miss something important we have not considered. It's obvious, for example, that in the natural sciences the scientific method is preferred:

Step 1: Question
Step 2: Research
Step 3: Hypothesize
Step 4: Experiment
Step 5: Observe
Step 6: Conclude
Step 7. Communicate/Replicate

This methodology is a reasonable approach to "knowing" in the natural sciences. It has taken us very far in our understanding of the natural world. But is this method the be-all-end-all type of knowledge in every circumstance? In their textbook *Research Methods in Psychology* the authors offer five ways of knowing that vie for space in the how we know areas of our minds, each with benefits and drawbacks, but nonetheless worth looking into when it comes to assessing how we take in and understand information and under what conditions and what circumstances. The following is a list of ways of knowing suggested by the authors. Below, I only give thumbnail definitions but I suggest going to the source to look up a complete explanation of each way of knowing:

1. **Intuition**—The first method of knowing is intuition. When we use our intuition, we are relying on our guts, our emotions, and/or our instincts to guide us. Rather than examining facts or using rational thought, intuition involves believing what feels true.

2. **Authority**—This method involves accepting new ideas because some authority figure states they are true. These authorities include parents, the media, doctors, priests and other religious authorities, the government, and professors.

3. **Rationalism**—Rationalism involves using logic and reasoning to acquire new knowledge. Using this method, premises are stated and logical rules are followed to arrive at sound conclusions.

4. **Empiricism**—Empiricism involves acquiring knowledge through observation and experience. We can only know some things by doing them.

5. **The Scientific Method** [168]

It's somewhat debatable as to the number of ways of knowing that exist. Some believe there is only one way of knowing. In the Western world, in particular, that tends to be through reason, but the number of ways of knowing also goes as high as eight in the Theory of Knowledge (TOK) course taught in the International Baccalaureate program. I thought I would just go with the psychologists on this one. So here we've just gone with the above five.

No matter how many ways of knowing we consider, each one adds to the end goal of *belief*. The first definition is an acceptance that a statement is true or that something exists. The second definition is trust, faith, or confidence in someone or something.[169] Here also is one definition of the *purpose of belief* from philosopher and psychoanalyst Jonathan Leicester: "to guide action, not to indicate truth. Decisions about actions often have to be made quickly in the absence of evidence."[170]

Once we accept something as true, we can't help but act on that belief. It could be as simple as establishing a conviction in our minds or the act of going off to war. The ladder of inference outlines the process that we go through to get to that action stage. No matter which way of knowing that's utilized, we arrive at the belief stage, and once arrived, we take our belief as true. Although in our minds we are seeking what we believe is an "objective truth," to a greater or lesser extent and often due to our own biases, we end up with subjective proofs, which are the result of our prior conditioning. At so many levels, even truth tends to be relative. So even though we remain in the world of subjectivity, we're hoping that these subjective answers we've arrived at for perceived problems will gradually whittle away at the mountain of uncertainty that lies just beneath the surface of our beliefs.

To avoid violent conflict we have learned to argue and discuss our differences, but our desire to win remains the ego-centered goal. Victory over the "other" is the most ego-satisfying outcome, and yet the philosophers say: "The aim of an argument or a discussion should not be victory but progress."[171] Progress is, after all, in our own "enlightened self-interest," for when we acknowledge the legitimate needs of others (or the interests of the group or groups to which they belong), we ultimately serve our interests.[172]

To do that we must be willing to try and see things from another person's point of view, even though any total understanding of that may be impossible, given the uniqueness of the other person or group, and that's where, again, compassion comes into the picture. We live in a time when science is validating what enlightened humans have known throughout the ages: that compassion is not a luxury; it is a necessity for our well-being, resilience, and survival.[173]

Separateness/Oneness

At one point, the evolutionary process demanded that we see ourselves as separate in order to survive. The more enlightened people on the planet need to see themselves as interconnected with the environment for the planet to survive. The ego's identification with separateness tends to make it see itself as more important than anything else, just as the mother will see her child as more important than someone else's child. That is basic evolutionary survival. We name and claim, but when we go beyond that place in our own awareness, we see all children as our children and all men and women as our brothers and sisters. We no longer reject the reality of the other person's human predicament and realize our *shared essence-of-being* which truly unites us.[174]

So, from this philosophical standpoint, there is no conflict with others because as the sage Ramana Maharshi said in answer to the question: How are we supposed to treat others? He replied, "There are no others." Or, as Eckhart Tolle has said about seeing others, it is just seeing yourself in another disguise. Connectedness and oneness with others is a step beyond the self-actualization that Maslow describes because it means transcending the individual separate ego-self. It inhabits that rare domain that few attain which the mystics would call *enlightenment.* It slips off the edge of our world of intellectual understanding because it can only be understood by experiencing it. Like that state of flow or deep meditation, we can only understand by doing. But this is natural: We cannot understand how it feels to ride a horse unless we ride the horse and no amount of florid language can transmit the feeling of being in love unless we have fallen in love or are in love.

Science is gradually discovering the evolutionary fabric of existence and it appears that there truly is a "moral arc" to evolution. Yes, it's true, if we look in the short term the world appears to be full of cruelty and suffering, but as Steven Pinker has shown in his book *Better Angels of our Nature*, violence has been on the decline for almost all of recorded history.[175]

From the amoeba to the human being we see the evidence of a long trajectory from selfishness (total ego identification) to selflessness (identification with the oneness of all existence) through kin selection, reciprocity, altruism, cooperation, and friendship. We have even seen some of these characteristics in interspecies relationships. So, having seen these things exist in the natural world as evidence of a hierarchical survival ladder of behavior, is it so unreasonable to assume that just a little way down the line loving our neighbor makes evolutionary sense? And taking one more step toward learning to love our enemy may also increase our survival chances as a species. After all, the British and Americans were once bitter enemies, having fought two wars against each other and are now the closest of allies. Perhaps in a very general way, there is a metaphor in all this that sits just below the surface. There are those "others" who are physically closest to us or appear to be so who, at the most basic level, we can come to care for because they look most like us. They may speak the same language or be from a close ethnic stock to ours. Those that look least like us make the process of identification more difficult. However, as we evolve as human beings, superficial outward appearances eventually give way to deeper identification parameters, like emotional and psychological disposition or perhaps cultural tastes and other similarities, which can only be recognized as we gradually get to know the other person.

When that happens, outward appearances begin to fall away and deeper understanding takes the place of the superficial likes or dislikes based on appearance. It's harder to dislike a person once we get to know them. That is perhaps why xenophobic groups try to keep those within the tribe from getting to know those outside the tribe. Mixing with those from other groups tends to weaken stereotyping. Friendships crossing ethnic and racial boundaries may ultimately lead to intermarriage. It's a fear held by many groups, especially those whose identities are based on narrow-minded premises. It's a numbers game. Anything that decreases our numbers decreases our power (hence our survivability). We've seen that tribalism break down with European immigrants over past generations and now more with different racial groups. At one time in the United States, there were many European ethnic organizations, particularly in all major cities that had substantial numbers of European immigrants: Italian American social clubs, Polish American social clubs, etc. They served as homes away from home for many immigrants. Gradually, however, succeeding generations saw little need to maintain the same relationships with those organizations, and today few remain.

One of the most heartening things taking place today in America is that the cutting edge of social and demographic change is being manifested in the mixed-race groups. They are not only the most tolerant; they are growing at a rate three times faster than the population as a whole. According to the Pew Research Center, 60% feel proud of their mixed-race background and also feel it has made them more open to other cultures.[176] Does all this mixing give us a better chance at surviving? If we go back over the history of species evolution it seems to bear this out. Let's remember it's not the biggest or the strongest who have survived but the most adaptable. Yes, in the short run, playing outside our group may be risky, but we are probably just ahead of the curve.

When we think of love isn't there a similar maturation arc of this emotion that seems to exist, beginning with our closest and dearest (i.e., kin including children, spouse, family) and depending on our capacity for identification and diminishing ego-self, the larger world and beyond?

Although psychologists have categorized love into familial love, romantic love, platonic love, etc., love in its most mature state has no other name but love. It exists beyond the need to differentiate. If we allow ourselves, it supports the oneness that we feel toward one another and all of existence. For some of us this feeling may only be a rare occurrence, but when it's there we know it and would like it to occur more often.

Consciousness

Does consciousness emerge from the brain or exist beyond the physical brain? This is the current science problem that holds a great deal of fascination across many fields of both science and philosophy. How do we know ourselves? How do we know we exist? Descartes's axiom, "I think therefore I am," doesn't give the mechanical details. And the devil is in the details.

In naming the problem, philosopher David Chalmers has coined the phrase *the hard problem of consciousness*, which he defines as "the problem of explaining why any physical state is conscious rather than non-conscious." The mysteries of consciousness are even getting mixed with quantum mechanics in an attempt to find answers as well as with numerous other theories, including the old philosophy of "Panpsychism," which holds that everything has some level of consciousness or mind ubiquitous in the universe.[177] This doesn't mean that all matter is self-aware but that there are levels of consciousness and simple forms like electrons and quarks that have extremely simple forms of experience, and the very complex forms like animals and humans derive their experience from the brain's most basic parts, leading to that self-awareness.[178]

Another philosophy both old and new, is the idea that consciousness is foundational to existence. Old in the sense that mystics have believed for thousands of years that matter emerges from consciousness; new in the sense that scientists like cognitive psychologist Donald Hoffman and others are attempting to prove that this is true by testing hypotheses using mathematical and psychophysical experiments.[179]

Two other researchers who have done a great deal of work in this area are Bernardo Kastrup and Robert Lanza. Kastrup, who has a Ph.D. in philosophy and another in computer engineering, is a leading thinker in the philosophy of "metaphysical idealism" and Lanza, a famous stem cell researcher, has written extensively (with theoretical physicist Matej Pavšič) on the subject of biocentrism, an ethical point of view that extends inherent value to all living things.[180] It also treats life and consciousness as pathways to understanding the essential nature of the universe.[181]

We can say that this is the direct opposite of materialist philosophy. "Materialism" is a form of philosophical monism that holds that matter is the fundamental substance in nature and that all things, including mental states and consciousness, are results of material interactions.[182] In other words, in materialism consciousness is an emergent state resulting from physical evolution.

These are simple thumbnail definitions of "idealism" and "materialism" and in no way can do justice to either philosophy, each having its history going back thousands of years; they are only intended as introductory notions. I would just say here that materialism and idealism or any of the other many -isms we can hang our hats upon, could, if we're not careful, become secondary sources of ego gratification, which often distract us from the simplicity of working on ourselves. It's the one thing we can do that requires nothing but our attention. No extra stuff needed.

Mindfulness

The Mayo Clinic defines mindfulness as "a type of meditation in which you focus on being intensely aware of what you're sensing and feeling in the moment, without interpretation or judgment. Practicing mindfulness involves breathing methods, guided imagery, and other practices to relax the body and mind and help reduce stress." They offer appointments to practice mindfulness and list the many benefits of the practice and how to do it. It looks like an excellent program.[183]

The mindfulness practices that have become so popular today, from yoga studios to some high-tech boardrooms, deserve to be appreciated for the good they can do, but the caution is that everything can become a fad. It can be a wonderful self-help tool like many forms of meditation, or it can be the hip and cool thing to at least say we are doing, serving more levels of ego gratification. Although, mindfulness meditation has been practiced in just about all the major religions for well over a thousand years, in the West we've associated it mostly with Buddhism and Hinduism, where we can trace it back over two thousand years.[184] But its practice as introduced in society today is mostly secular. And we might say that for its critics this is one of the problems, since they believe the value of the practice has been compromised and monetized by those who would exploit its benefits to make more efficient worker bees for business. I would only say that most beneficial practices have the possibility of being exploited and, in that regard, there is nothing new under the sun. So let's not throw the baby out with the bathwater.

Perhaps the biggest influence in bringing mindfulness to the West was Jon Kabat-Zinn who, in 1979, founded the Oasis Institute for Mindfulness, which is the Mindfulness-Based Professional Education and Training Center at the University of Massachusetts Medical School. Kabat-Zinn studied under several Buddhist teachers, including Thich Nhat Hanh, who is an influential mindfulness teacher himself. This gave Kabat-Zinn a foundation in mindfulness that he then integrated with

Western science to develop Mindfulness-Based Stress Reduction Therapy (MBSR). For a society unfamiliar with Eastern practices, this more secular approach made it more acceptable.[185]

Mindfulness meditation also turns out to be an effective treatment for mood and anxiety disorders as well as emotion regulation ability. In studies it has also turned out to be superior to Cognitive Behavior Therapy (CBT) for these problems. The results show that by accepting thoughts and feelings without judgment and learning to focus on the present moment, mindfulness meditation exerts effects of enhanced self-regulation, including attention control, emotion regulation, and self-awareness.[186]

One recent neurological study that focused on mindful attention to breath showed how the exercises helped integrate the amygdala with the prefrontal cortex, resulting in emotion regulation.[187] A brief mindfulness meditation exercise is provided in Appendix 3. The practice of mindfulness is a useful tool to negotiate the difficulties of self-inquiry. Without the capacity to objectively look at ourselves (as mindfulness helps us do), surviving in a complex world is far more difficult. Because we are naturally concerned with what others think of us, how we view ourselves is dependent on our capacity for objectivity.

Mindfulness is awareness that arises through paying attention, on purpose, in the present moment, non-judgmentally.... And then I sometimes add, in the service of self-understanding and wisdom.[188]
~ John Kabat-Zinn

Survival is the prime directive and fear is the response to survival threats. Biology and neuroscience now tell us what the chemistry is doing in our brains, so we know much more about the mechanics of why we behave the way we do. However, isn't it useful to investigate what our minds and bodies are capable of doing on their own? I in no way want to minimize the great advances and help that science has to offer. But science itself gives us proofs that many ancient traditional practices can be extremely useful on our own journey of self-discovery, the benefits of meditation, for example, so why not take advantage of them?

Those proofs that science offers can only be realized by practice, not solely through an intellectual understanding.

Pure logical thinking cannot yield us any knowledge of the empirical world; all knowledge of reality starts from experience and ends in it.[189]

~ Albert Einstein

Just as love can only be understood by loving, there is the experience and the experiencer: Both are necessary for awareness to occur.

Summary

So, is there any through-line that connects the dots? How are all these headings and subheadings connected? The survivability of humankind by way of the individual self is integrated with the collective whole. And, by extension, not just the human condition, but that of all sentient beings. So, until we recognize our connection and interdependence with the rest of the sentient travelers on this evolutionary journey, our trajectory as a species will not be to survive but to self-destruct along with every other living thing around us. Well, possibly not cockroaches, they may yet inherit the earth.

There is one philosophical construct, which says that the cell is to the body what the body is to the planet, and the planet is to the galaxy, ad infinitum. It's both New Age and an ancient philosophical idea. But no matter how erudite the philosophical speculation about the nature of the cosmos, it does little to help us be kind, compassionate, and loving to our fellow human beings. That, ultimately, takes self-inquiry and working through relationships. Life is always our best teacher in that regard and, thankfully, if we keep our eyes open, many helpful and inspiring individuals come along to help us on our way.

It's my hope that the many subjects touched on in this book have shown that we can look at every aspect of our being with a deeper awareness, and that the narrower the view we have of ourselves and who we are, the smaller the window out of which we see the world. As we expand that sense of self, the more of existence we embrace.

The outline for this book has been Maslow's Hierarchy of Human Needs with support from other philosophies and outlines, including Lawrence Kohlberg's and Jane Loevinger's moral and ego-development theories. Some of the writings may have resonated with you and some may not have. I can only say that these observations have made some sense to me over my lifetime and I'm just grateful to be experiencing this period in my life when it's allowed me to write some of it down.

One of Martin Luther King Jr's favorite quotes was by the nineteenth-century Unitarian minister Theodore Parker who said, "The arc of the moral universe is long, but it bends toward justice." Might this also be an evolutionary dictum? Isn't it simply possible that this "long moral arc" is imbedded, to some degree, in our DNA? We've shown how at least some aspects of moral behavior appear to have developed in our primate cousins. We, in our turn, have managed to carry it further down the road of civility, if not always consistently. But, if we were to take a step beyond justice and toward advancing awareness, we would find compassion available to extend to our fellow planetary citizens, and perhaps, just a step beyond that, we would discover love. These steps are not at all fanciful, but simply the natural evolutionary progress of enlightened conscious awareness, and that awareness may, in the end, be all that survives.

Conclusion

In speaking of the ego-self the sage Nisargadatta Maharaj said:

Self-interest and self-concern are the focal points of the false. Your daily life vibrates between desire and fear. Watch it intently and you will see how the mind assumes innumerable names and shapes, like a river foaming between boulders. Trace every action to its selfish motive and look at the motive intently until it dissolves.... Discard every self-seeking motive as soon as it is seen and you need not look for truth; truth will find you.[190]

The thesis for this book is on the surface simple: Survival is the prime directive for all living organisms. That is nothing new to just about anyone. The realization of that simple truth, once recognized, however, is usually put on the back shelf of our subconscious and left there while other seemingly more important concerns are addressed. What I've tried to do in this book is suggest that there are no concerns that are more important; this desire to survive should be at the forefront of our conscious minds since it is the underlying motivation for all we do. From conception to death and perhaps beyond that simple directive is the driver for all thought and action. In the end, it is the ego-self or the false self that is driven to survive. It is that self, which we believe to be who we are, and which defines our existence. Not until we recognize it for what it is, can we let it go and become much more. Some might say that this is all just another illusion and just a play within a play and perhaps they are right. But don't peace, joy, and love outweigh attachment and suffering? Isn't that realization alone worth the journey of self-discovery?

Yesterday I was clever, so I wanted to change the world. Today I am wise, so I am changing myself.

~ Rumi

Appendix 1

The Prisoner's Dilemma

Two members of a criminal gang are arrested and imprisoned. Each prisoner is in solitary confinement with no means of communicating with the other. The prosecutors lack sufficient evidence to convict the pair on the principal charge, but they have enough to convict both on a lesser charge. Simultaneously, the prosecutors offer each prisoner a bargain. Each prisoner is given the opportunity either to betray the other by testifying that the other committed the crime or to cooperate with the other by remaining silent. The possible outcomes are:

- If A and B each betray the other, each of them serves two years in prison.
- If A betrays B but B remains silent, A will be set free and B will serve three years in prison.
- If A remains silent but B betrays A, A will serve three years in prison and B will be set free.
- If A and B both remain silent, both of them will serve only one year in prison (on the lesser charge).

Kuhn, S., "Prisoner's Dilemma", *The Stanford Encyclopedia of Philosophy* (Winter 2019 Edition), Edward N. Zalta (ed.), URL = <https://plato.stanford.edu/archives/win2019/entries/prisoner-dilemma/>.

Appendix 2

Explanation of Ethical Theories

Ethical schools:

"Deontology: Its name comes from the Greek word *deon*, meaning duty. Actions that obey these rules are ethical, while actions that do not, are not. This ethical theory is most closely associated with German philosopher Immanuel Kant." https://ethics.org.au/ethics-explainer-deontology/

"Utilitarianism is an ethical theory that determines right from wrong by focusing on outcomes. It is a form of consequentialism. Utilitarianism holds that the most ethical choice is the one that will produce the greatest good for the greatest number. It is the only moral framework that can be used to justify military force or war. It is also the most common approach to moral reasoning used in business because of the way in which it accounts for costs and benefits. However, because we cannot predict the future, it's difficult to know with certainty whether the consequences of our actions will be good or bad. This is one of the limitations of utilitarianism." https://ethicsunwrapped.utexas.edu/glossary/utilitarianism.

"Virtue ethics is a philosophy developed by Aristotle and other ancient Greeks. It is the quest to understand and live a life of moral character. This character-based approach to morality assumes that we acquire virtue through practice. By practicing being honest, brave, just, generous, and so on, a person develops an honorable and moral character. According to Aristotle, by honing virtuous habits, people will likely make the right choice when faced with ethical challenges." https://ethicsunwrapped.utexas.edu/glossary/virtue-ethics

The following is simply a list of some of the other popular ethical theories:

- Ethics of care.
- Egoism.
- Religion or Divine Command Theory.
- Natural Law.
- Social Contract Theory.

Appendix 3

One Example of a Mindfulness Meditation Exercise

There are many types of meditation. For our purposes we will focus on mindfulness meditation and offer a simple exercise. There are many wonderful teachers and books on the subject. This particular exercise comes from the Living Well organization.

"Background: The purpose of this exercise is to simply notice, accept and be aware of your breath – it is not about relaxation or stress reduction, although this may well occur. Breathing is something we all do – if you have a pulse then you breathe. Your body knows how to do this; it has done it since birth. This is simply about breathing mindfully. Breathing is something you carry with you everywhere; you are just not usually aware of it.

"Sit quietly in a chair with both feet on the ground and your hands in your lap. Allow yourself to feel centered in the chair. Bring all of your attention to the physical act of breathing. Start to notice the breath as it enters your body through your nose and travels to your lungs. Notice with curiosity whether the inward and outward breaths are cool or warm, and notice where the breath travels as it enters and departs.

"Also notice the breath as your lungs relax and you inhale through your nose. Don't try to do anything with your breathing – simply notice it, pay attention to it and be aware of it. It doesn't matter if your breathing is slow or fast, deep or shallow; it just is what it is. Allow your body to do what it does naturally.

"You will start to notice that each time you breathe in, your diaphragm or stomach will expand... and each time you breathe out your diaphragm or stomach will relax. Again, don't try to do anything – just be aware of the physical sensations of breathing in and breathing out. If you find that thoughts intrude, this is okay. Don't worry, just notice the thoughts, allow them to be, and gently bring your awareness back to your breath.

"Start this exercise initially for 5 minutes, building up daily. You can also do this exercise lying down in bed if you have difficulty sleeping. It is simply a way of allowing you to have more mindful and conscious awareness of your body and its surroundings, its breathing and its capacity to relax. When our breathing relaxes our muscles relax."

https://www.livingwell.org.au/wp-content/uploads/2012/11/5-BreathingMindfulness.pdf

Those who are new to the practice of meditation generally find it useful to hear instructions of this kind spoken aloud, in the form of a guided meditation. UCLA's *Mindful Awareness Research Center* has several which beginners should find helpful.

Endnotes

Introduction

1   McLeod, S. (2020, December 29). Maslow's Hierarchy of Needs. *Simply Psychology*. https://www.simplypsychology.org/maslow.html

2   Maslow, A. (2013). A Theory of Human Motivation. *Martino Publishing*. Mansfield Centre CT. p.14

3   Herndon, E. (2018, February 6). What are multiple intelligences and how do they affect learning? [Web log post]. Retrieved from https://www.cornerstone.edu/blogs/lifelong-learning-matters/post/what-are-multiple-intelligences-and-how-do-they-affect-learning

Chapter 1

4   Brakin, J. (2016. April 22). Life Will Out – What Will You Leave this world. *Someday Is Now*. https://somedayisnow.me/life-will-out-what-will-you-leave-this-world/

5   Gildenhuys, P. (2019). "Natural Selection", *The Stanford Encyclopedia of Philosophy* (Winter 2019 Edition), Edward N. Zalta (ed.), URL = <https://plato.stanford.edu/archives/win2019/entries/natural-selection/>.

6   Survival. (n.d.). In Merriam-webster.com dictionary. Retrieved from https://www.merriam-webster.com/dictionary/survival

7   Bekoff, M. (2017, November 21) Animals Aren't Sentient and Can't Feel Pain, Tories Claim. *Psychology Today*. https://www.psychologytoday.com/us/blog/animal-emotions/201711/animals-arent-sentient-and-cant-feel-pain-tories-claim

8   Gopnik, A. (2020, July 23). Learning without a brain. *Wall Street Journal* https://www.wsj.com/articles/learning-without-a-brain-11595527115

9   Xinhua. (2019, September 16). Unicellular organisms can learn, remember:Israeli-Spanish research *XINHUANET*. http://www.xinhuanet.com/english/2019-09/16/c_1383 93828.htm

10   CNRS. (2016, April 27). A single-celled organism capable of learning. *ScienceDaily*. Retrieved August 11, 2020 from www.sciencedaily.com/releases/2016/04/160427081533. htm

11   Hoff, M. (2020, November 12). Information Gained, Stored, and Transferred Without Brains. *ask nature*. https://askna-ture.org/strategy/brainless-slime-molds-both-learn-and-teach/

12   Ibid.

13   Williams, R. (2019. December 5). Single-Celled Organism Appears to Make Decisions. *The Scientist*. https://www. the-scientist.com/news-opinion/single-celled-organism-appears-to-make decisions-66818

14   Ibid.

15   Ibid.

16   Ibid.

17   Rossine, et al. (2020, March 19). Eco-evolutionary significance of "loners." *Plos Biology*. Retrieved from https://jour-nals.plos.org/plosbiology/article?id=10.1371%2Fjournal. pbio.3000642&fbclid=IwAR0QTM3osZJiJY9_9IUzDlfSV8x Hf5kkAI6d1aG33PODN-IuiblnfS1tyTE

18   Steimer, T. (2002. September 4). The biology of-fear-and anxiety. *National Library of Medicine*. https://pubmed.ncbi. nlm.nih.gov/22033741/#affiliation-1

19   Levin, M. (2020, October,13). Cognition all the way down. *Aeon*.   https://aeon.co/essays/how-to-understand-cells-tissues-and-organisms-as-agents-with-agendas?utm_ source=Aeon+Newsletter&utm_campaign=c3aa091573-EMAIL_CAMPAIGN_2020_10_16_01_06&utm_ medium=email&utm_term=0_411a82e59d-

c3aa091573-70902379

20 Ibid; Animal Sentience (2016). https://animalstudiesrepository.org/animsent/

21 Anderson, R. (2019, March). A Journey into the Animal Mind. *The Atlantic.* https://www.theatlantic.com/magazine/archive/2019/03/what-the-crow-knows/580726/

22 Woodruff, M. (2020. July 3). Do fish have faces? *Aeon.* https://aeon.co/essays/fish-are-nothing-like-us-except-that-they-are-sentient-being

23 Ibid.

24 Ibid.

25 Gildenhuys, P. (2019). "Natural Selection", *The Stanford Encyclopedia of Philosophy* (Winter 2019 Edition), Edward N. Zalta (ed.), URL = Available from: <https://plato.stanford.edu/archives/win2019/entries/natural-selection/>.

26 Hogenboom, M. (2016, August 23). Why bullying is such a successful evolutionary strategy. *Earth.* http://www.bbc.com/earth/story/20160822-why-bullying-is-such-a-successful-evolutionary-strategy

27 George, J. (2006. February 17). Polar bear no match for fearsome mother in Ivujivik. *Numatsiaq News.* https://science.howstuffworks.com/life/inside-the-mind/human-brain/how-stress-works.htm

28 Sapolsky, R. (2017). *Behave: The Biology of Humans at Our Best and Worst.* Penguin.

29 Schmidt, M. (2020. March 13). Why Coronavirus Is Turning People into Hoarders: A Q&A on the Psychology of Pandemics. *Discover.* https://www.discovermagazine.com/health/why-coronavirus-is-turning-people-into-hoarders-a-q-and-a-on-the-psychology

30 Plant Behaviour & Cognition | Monica Gagliano | Scientific Research https://www.monicagagliano.com

31 Shaeffer, l. (2020, august 23) The most successful strategy in life. *The Pennsylvania Capitol Star.* https://www.penncap-

ital-star.com/commentary/the-most-successful-strategy-in-life-lloyd-e-sheaffer/

32 Schultz, N. (2007. June 25). Altruistic chimps act for the benefit of others. *New Scientist*. https://www.newscientist. com/article/dn12132-altruistic-chimps-act-for-the-benefit-of-others/

33 Animal Behaviour: Abbott, A. (2015, May 26). Inside the cunning, caring and greedy minds of fish. *Nature*. https://www.nature.com/news/animal-behaviour-inside-the-cunning-caring-and-greedy-minds-of-fish-1.17614?WT. ec_id=NATURE-20150528

34 Nowak, M. and Roch, S. (2007, March 7). Upstream reciprocity and the evolution of gratitude. *National Center Biotechnological Information*. https://www.ncbi.nlm.nih.gov/ pmc/articles/PMC2197219/

35 Schultz, N. (2007. June 25). Altruistic chimps act for the benefit of others. *New Scientist*. https://www.newscientist. com/article/dn12132-altruistic-chimps-act-for-the-benefit-of-others/

36 Sapolsky, R. (2006, April 6). The 2% Difference. *Discover Mag*. https://www.discovermagazine.com/planet-earth/ the-2-difference

37 Ibid.

38 Dingman, M. (2014. May 17). Know Your Brain: Prefrontal cortex. Neuroscientific ally Challenged. https://www.neuroscientificallychallenged.com/blog/2014/5/16/know-your-brain-prefrontal-cortex

39 Koch, C. (2018 June 1). What Is Consciousness. *Scientific American*. https://www.scientificamerican.com/article/what-is-consciousness/

40 Vaupel. J. (2018. January 23). Women live longer than men even during severe famines and epidemics. *PNAS*. https:// www.pnas.org/content/115/4/E832

41 Cahill, L. (2012. October 1). His Brain Her Brain. *Scientific*

American. https://www.scientificamerican.com/article/his-brain-her-brain-2012-10-23/

42 Morell, V (2017. February 13). Monkeys master a key sign of self-awareness: recognizing their reflections. *Science.* https://www.sciencemag.org/news/2017/02/monkeys-master-key-sign-self-awareness-recognizing-their-reflections

43 Suarez, S. Pacey, A (2005. November 04). Sperm transport in the female reproductive tract. *Human Reproduction Update.* https://academic.oup.com/humupd/article/12/1/23/607817

44 Bellefonds, C. (2020. May 14). Why Michael Phelps Has the Perfect Body for Swimming. *Biography.* https://www.biography.com/news/michael-phelp-perfect-body-swimming

45 Smith, E. (2015. December 2). Is Human Morality A Product of Evolution? *The Atlantic.* https://www.theatlantic.com/health/archive/2015/12/evolution-of-morality-social-humans-and-apes/418371/

46 Stierwalt, R. (2020, April 4) How Can You Tell if You Have Perfect Pitch. *Scientific American.* https://www.scientificamerican.com/article/how-can-you-tell-if-you-have-perfect-pitch/

47 Rice, C. (2015, June 24). A Nation that still falls short of its ideals. *The Baltimore Sun.* https://www.baltimoresun.com/opinion/readers-respond/bs-ed-racism-letter-20150624-story.html

48 Cherry, K. (2020. June 29). Overview of the 6 Major Theories of Emotion. *Verywell Mind.* https://www.verywellmind.com/theories-of-emotion-2795717

49 Smith, E. *Is human morality a product of evolution?*

50 Darwin, C.R. (1871) The Descent of Man.

51 DeWall, Franz. (2005, September 1). The Evolution of Empathy. *Greater Good Magazine.* https://greatergood.berkeley.edu/article/item/the_evolution_of_empathy

52 Biological Foundations of Morality. (2010, March 18–19). *McFarland Center for Religion Ethics and Culture.https://*

www.holycross.edu/faith-service/mcfarland-center-religion-ethics-and-culture/conferences/biological-foundations

53   "The Origins of Virtue – Summary" eNotes Publishing Ed. eNotes Editorial. eNotes.com, Inc.eNotes.com 1 August, 2020 http://www.enotes.com/topics/origins-virtue #summary-summary-855912

54   Hawking, S and Mlodinow, L. (2010, October 1). The Elusive Theory of Everything. Scientific American. https://www.scientificamerican.com/article/the-elusive-thoery-of-everything/

55   Haidt, J. (2008). Morality. *Perspectives On Psychological Science.* https://people.stern.nyu.edu/jhaidt/articles/haidt.2008.morality.pub052.pdf

56   Ibid. p.70

57   Holt, J. (2011, November 25). Two Brains Running. *New York Times.* https://www.nytimes.com/2011/11/27/books/review/thinking-fast-and-slow-by-daniel-kahneman-book-review.html

58   Haidt, J. (2006). The Happiness Hypothesis: finding Modern truth in ancient wisdom. New York, Basic Books pp.4–5.

59   Haidt, J. (2013). The Righteous Mind: Why Good People Are Divided by Politics and Religion. New York. Vintage Books. p71.

60   Ibid.

61   Ibid p.72.

62   Travis, C and Aronson, E. (2007). Mistakes Were Made (but not by me). Boston, Mariner Books. pp. 15–18

63   Kaufman, C. (2012, August 12). Why Bad Guys Think They're Good Guys. *Psychology Today.* https://www.psychologytoday.com/us/blog/psychology-writers/201208/why-bad-guys-think-theyre-good-guys

64   Blumenfeld, R. (2020, March 21). How a 15,000-Year-Old

Human Bone Could Help You through the Coronacrisis. *Forbes.* https://www.forbes.com/sites/remyblumenfeld/2020/03/21/how-a-15000-year-old-human-bone-could-help-you-through-the--coronavirus/#d32569637e9b

Chapter 2

65 (2021, April 28). Hero's Journey: Definition and Step-by-Step Guide. *Reedsyblog.* https://blog.reedsy.com/guide/story-structure/heros-journey/

66 Milton, J. (2000). Paradise Lost. New York, NY: Penguin Books.

67 Priebe, H. (2015, May 13). Be the Anti-Hero of Your Own Life. Thought Catalog. Retrieved from. https://thoughtcatalog.com/heidi-priebe/2015/05/be-the-anti-hero-of-your-own-life/

68 Konnikova, M. (2015, June 12.) The Real Lesson of the Stanford Prison Experiment. The New Yorker. https://www.newyorker.com/science/maria-konnikova/the-real-lesson-of-the-stanford-prison-experiment.

69 Dash, M. (2011, December 23). The Story of the WWI Christmas Truce. Smithsonian Magazine. https://www.smithsonianmag.com/history/the-story-of-the-wwi-christmas-truce-11972213/

70 Tartakovsky, M. (2018, July 8). Owning Our dark Sides. Psych Central. https://psychcentral.com/blog/owning-our-dark-sides/.

71 Rey, G. (2020, August 8). Philosophy of Mind. Encyclopedia Britannica. Retrieved August 17, 2020, from (https://www.britannica.com/topic/philosophy-of-mind

72 C.G. Jung, *Collected Works*, vol. 6, paragraph 643.

73 C. G. Jung, "Introduction," *Collected Works*, vol. 12, para. 44.

74 Rodriquez, E. (2018, Nov. 16). Ego. The Encyclopedia Britannica. Retrieved from https://www.britannica.com/top-

ic/ego-philosophy-and-psychology.

75 Platts-Mills, B. (2020, October 20). Memory involves the whole body. Psyche https://psyche.co/ideas/memory-involves-the-whole-body-its-how-the-self-defies-amnesia?fbclid=IwAR1YzGcDvLC6ASSQFkt6I_mEAzfsa2zg9NcQ_BLHnRDikNRQmB2Vlyx4a5c

76 Cherry, K. (2020, June 25). The Origins of Psychology. Very Well Mind. Retrieved from https://www.verywellmind.com/a-brief-history-of-psychology-through-the-years-2795245

77 Merriam-Webster. (n.d.). Ego. In Merriam-Webster.com dictionary. Retrieved August 17, 2020, from https://www.merriam-webster.com/dictionary/ego.

78 Cherry, K. (2019, September 28). Freud's Id, Ego, and Superego. Very Well Mind. https://www.verywellmind.com/the-id-ego-and-superego-2795951

79 Smith, E. (2015, December 2). Is Human Morality a Product of Evolution. *The Atlantic.* https://www.theatlantic.com/health/archive/2015/12/evolution-of-morality-social-humans-and-apes/418371/

80 (2014, May 14). Lucky Age 7: why and How kids Change. Education.com. Retrieved September 3, 2020, from https://www.education.com/magazine/article/Lucky_7._

81 Cherry, K. Freud's Id.

82 Sachs, S. (1998, August 16). Age of Reason; A chilling Crime and a Question: What's in a child's mind? *The New York Times.* Retrieved from https://www.nytimes.com/1998/08/16/weekinreview/the-age-of-reason-a-chilling-crime-and-a-question-what-s-in-a-child-s-mind.html

83 Cherry, K. Freud's. Id.

84 Mohammed, H. (2020, February 28). Why do girls mature faster than boys? *Baron News.* https://www.baronnews.com/2020/02/28/why-do-girls-mature-faster-than-boys/

85 Haidt, J. (2012). The Righteous Mind. 72. New York, NY:

Vintage Books.

86 Pederson, D. (2020, August 18). Perception, Medium. (https://medium.com/personal-growth/perception-ca058251e197

87 Wadi'h, H. (2004, December 10). When does 2+2 not equal 4? People's World. https://www.peoplesworld.org/article/when-does-2-2-not-equal-4/.

88 Merenus, M. (2020, June 9). Gardner's Theory of Multiple Intelligences. *Simply Psychology.* https://www.simplypsychology.org/multiple-intelligences.html

89 Johns Hopkins University. (2020, June 8). Philosophy lab. Test' finds objective vision impossible. Medical Press. https://medicalxpress.com/news/2020-06-philosophy-lab-vision-impossible.html.

90 Boogaard, K. (2019, June 18).

91 Toggle Track. https://toggl.com/blog/ladder-of-inference.

92 Itzhak, F. et. al. (2020, June). Internally Generated Preactivation of Single Neurons in Human Medial Frontal Cortex Predicts Volition. p.548. Cell Press. http://braininstprd.wpengine.com/wp-content/uploads/2020/06/gk2630.pdf.

93 Keeton, CP, et al. (2008, April 22). Sense of Control Predicts Depressive and Anxious Symptoms Across the Transition to Parenthood. PMC. https://www.ncbi.nlm.nih.gov/pmc/articles/PMC2834184/

94 Gholipour, B. (2019, March 21). Philosophers and neuroscientists join forces to see whether science can solve the mystery of free will. Science Magazine. https://www.sciencemag.org/news/2019/03/philosophers-and-neuroscientists-join-forces-see-whether-science-can-solve-mystery-free?utm_campaign=SciMag&utm_source=JHubbard&utm_medium=Facebook

95 https://pubmed.ncbi.nlm.nih.gov/6640273/

96 Soon, C.S. et al. (2008, June). Unconscious determinants of free decisions in the human brain. Research Gate. https://

www.researchgate.net/publication/5443390_Unconscious_
determinants_of_free_decisions_in_the_human_brain.

97   Harris, S. (2012, p.9). Free Will. New York, NY. Free Press.

98   Kahn, N., and Shen, J. (2020, February 20). Brian Greene
      talks about the Physics of Free Will at the Science Center
      Lecture. The Harvard Crimson. J.https://www.thecrimson.
      com/article/2020/2/20/brian-greene-physics-will/.

99   Goldhill, O. (2015, September 20). Neuroscience backs up
      the Buddhist belief that "the self" isn't constant but ever-
      changing. Quartz. https://qz.com/506229/neuroscience-
      backs-up-the-buddhist-belief-that-the-self-isnt-constant-
      but-ever-changing/.

100   Ibid.

101   Gholipour, B. (2019, September 10). A Famous Argument
      Against Free Will. *The Atlantic.* https://www.theatlantic.
      com/health/archive/2019/09/free-will-bereitschaftspoten-
      tial/597736/

102   Shaun, N. (2008, August 19). Free Will versus the Pro-
      grammed Brain. Scientific American. https://www.scienti-
      ficamerican.com/article/free-will-vs-programmed-brain/

103   Ibid.

104   Reynolds, E. (2020, October 20). After Cheating on a Test,
      People Claim to Have Known the Answers Anyway. Re-
      search Digest. https://digest.bps.org.uk/2020/10/20/after-
      cheating-on-a-test-people-claim-to-have-known-the-an-
      swers-anyway/?fbclid=IwAR0bVvQIjJh4j1k1c3Y_9w1mEq
      NuXkZPSGm9LSc_tXxTXirX328EXZCGTQM.

105   Ibid.

106   Todd Solondz Read more at https://www.brainyquote.
      com/topics/survival.

107   Bruss, J. (2018, October 31). Quora. https://www.quora.
      com/Are-humans-manipulative-by-nature

108   Oakley D. Halligan, P. (2017, November 14). Chasing the
      Rainbow: The Non-conscious Nature of Being. Frontiers in

Psychology. https://www.frontiersin.org/articles/10.3389/fpsyg.2017.01924/full

109 Ibid.

110 Resnick, B. (2018, June 6). The "marshmallow test" said patience was a key to success. A new replication tells us s'more. Vox. Retrieved from https://www.vox.com/science-and-health/2018/6/6/17413000/marshmallow-test-replication-mischel-psychology.

111 Ibid.

112 (Merriam-Webster. (n.d.). Fatalism. In Merriam-Webster.com dictionary. Retrieved January 3, 2021, from https://www.merriam-webster.com/dictionary/fatalism.

113 The Editors of Encyclopedia Britannica. (2020, January 31). Determinism. Encyclopedia Britannica. Retrieved from https://www.britannica.com/topic/determinism. January 03, 2021

114 (2006 April 26). Compatibilism. Stanford Encyclopedia of Philosophy. https://plato.stanford.edu/entries/compatibilism/.

115 Woolley, D, and Ghossainy, M. (2013, September) revisiting the Fantasy-Reality Distinction: Children as Naïve Skeptics. PMC. https://www.ncbi.nlm.nih.gov/pmc/articles/PMC3689871/

116 Ibid.

117 Ibid.

118 Oakley D. Halligan, P. (2017, November 17) What if consciousness is not what drives the human mind. The Conversation. Retrieved from https://theconversation.com/what-if-consciousness-is-not-what-drives-the-human-mind-86785.

119 Haidt, The Righteous Mind p86.

120 Ibid. p. 90.

121 Ibid. p. 96.

122 Ibid. p. 91.

123 Lewis Thomas Read more at https://www.brainyquote. com/topics/survival

124 Kolbert, E. (2017, February 20). Why Facts Don't Change Our Minds. New Yorker. https://www.newyorker.com/magazine/2017/02/27/why-facts-dont-change-our-minds?fbclid=IwAR3FDr_OsE22OFivtjTnaBl6pl37x14oSn-BANtGlVShLa8uj8Kl3pyFmCi8

125 Dolan, E. (2019, August 23). Ingroup – versus – outgroup thinking warps the moral principles of liberals and conservatives. PsyPost.https://www.psypost.org/2019/08/ingroup-versus-outgroup-thinking-warps-the-moral-principles-of-liberals-and-conservatives-54277

126 Harari Y. (2020 September 13). Why Fascsim is so tempting. Ted Ed. YouTube. https://ed.ted.com/lessons/why-fascism-is-so-tempting-and-how-your-data-could-power-it-yuval-noah-harari?fbclid=IwAR3JSJaGsxAfpP4hUjdUmhWjKQkJyejrFh2H-itQlIBKi40loQ0UCt4GUu0

127 Lost Connections... Johann Hari p.77

128 Ibid.

129 Ibid. p. 83

130 Bloom, P. (2016) Against Empathy. Harper Collins. New York. p.94.

131 (Lannotti, 1978).

132 Clabough, E. (2016, March 4). Survival of the Most Empathetic. Psychology Today. https://www.psychologytoday.com/us/blog/neuroparent/201603/survival-the-most-empathetic

133 Lubetzky, D. Read more at https://www.brainyquote.com/topics/survival

134 Browning, C. (1998). Ordinary Men. Harper Perennial. New York.

135 Fromm, E. (1964) The Heart of Man. Harper and Row. New York p. 80.

136 Merkur, D. (2010, January) Erich Fromm' Human-

istic Psychoanalysist. *Brill.* https://brill.com/view/
book/9789042028609/B9789042028609-s005.xml

137 Heart of Man p. 86.

138 Ibid. 92.

139 Ibid. pp. 106–109.

140 The Conversation. (March 17, 2021). Selfish or Selfless. *Neuroscience News.* https://neurosciencenews.com/human-nature-selfish-selfless-18057/?fbclid=IwAR3gZk4ke-CH-nEQza6BJ8QfFTGjOWE_UcsceHqXF78k_fyO79S7AQViu-Mu4

Chapter 3

141 Righteous Mind, Haidt. p. 72.

142 Darwin C. (1859) p 537

143 Asma, S. (2014, November 11). United by Feelings. *Aeon.* https://aeon.co/essays/human-culture-and-cognition-evolved-through-the-emotions

144 Ibid.

145 Penn State. (2019, February 25). Some personal beliefs and morals may stem from genetics. *Science News.*

146 Lawrence Kohlberg. Blog Last Update: 07-06-2015. https://www.goodtherapy.org/famous-psychologists/lawrence-kohlberg.html

147 Barger, R. (2000). A Summary of Lawrence Kohlberg's Stages of Moral Development. https://www.qcc.cuny.edu/SocialSciences/ppecorino/MEDICAL_ETHICS_TEXT/Chapter_2_Ethical_Traditions/Reading-Barger-on-Kohlberg.htm

148 Suchman, N. PhD et al. Ego Development Psychopathology, and Parenting Problems in Substance-Abusing Mothers. *National Center for Biotechnology Information.* https://www.ncbi.nlm.nih.gov/pmc/articles/PMC2729054/

149 Ibid.

150 Loevinger, J. (2020, January 31). The Stages of Ego Devel-

opment Theory according to Jane Loevinger. *American Institute for Learning and Human Development*. Retrieved from https://www.institute4learning.com/2020/01/31/the-stages-of-ego-development-according-to-jane-loevinger/.

151 Cook-Greuter, S. (2013, December) Nine Levels of Increasing Embrace in Ego Development: a Full-Spectrum Theory Of Vertical Growth And Meaning Making. *Goodreads*. http://www.cook-greuter.com/Cook-Greuter%209%20levels%20paper%20new%201.1%2714%2097p%5B1%5D.pdft

152 Ibid.

153 Schoenherr, N. (2020, March 6). Book explores "rugged individualism" and its impact on inequality in America. *The Source*. Retrieved from https://source.wustl.edu/2020/03/book-explores-rugged-individualism-and-its-impact-on-inequality-in-america/

154 Bourg Carter, S. (2012, January 31). 6 Reasons You Should Spend More Time Alone. *Psychology Today*. https://www.psychologytoday.com/us/blog/high-octane-women/201201/6-reasons-you-should-spend-more-time-alone

155 Klien, E. (2017, February 28). Yuval Harari, author of Sapiens, on how meditation made him a better historian https://www.vox.com/2017/2/28/14745596/yuval-harari-sapiens-interview-meditation-ezra-klein

156 Lucas, M. (2010, June 30). Why Independence Isn't Worth The Fireworks. *Psychology Today*. https://www.psychologytoday.com/us/blog/rewire-your-brain-love/201006/why-independence-isnt-worth-the-fireworks

157 Ibid.

158 Ibid.

159 Briet, C. (2018, August 27). How to know it's Time to Let Go of Someone You Love. *Time*. https://time.com/5373451/break-up-someone-love/

160 Rayner, T. (2008, April 7). Heraclitus, change and flow. *Phi-

losophy for Change. Retrieved from https://philosophyfor-change.wordpress.com/2008/04/07/heraclitus-on-change/

161 Cook-Greuter, S. (2013, December)

162 Csikszentmihalyi, M. (2004, February) *Flow, the secret to happiness.* [Video file] Retrieved from https://www.ted. com/talks/mihaly_csikszentmihalyi_flow_the_secret_to_ happiness/transcript?language=en

163 Ibid.

164 Depersonalization-derealization disorder. (n.d.) *Mayo Clinic.* Retrieved from https://www.mayoclinic.org/diseas-es-conditions/depersonalization-derealization-disorder/symptoms-causes/syc-20352911.

165 The Cross-Eyed Pianist. (2020, May 25). A state of ecsta-sy: flow. *The Cross-Eyed Pianist.* https://crosseyedpianist. com/2020/05/25/a-state-of-ecstasy-flow/.

166 Kotler, Steven. (n.d.) Frequently Asked Questions on Flow. Retrieved from https://www.stevenkotler.com/rabbit-hole/ frequently-asked-questions-on-flo Cherry, K. (2020, June 3). Flow Can Help You Achieve Goals. *Verywellmind.* htt-ps://www.verywellmind.com/what-is-flow-2794768

167 Samayoa, W. (2020, Nov. 20). Why You Should Build a Healthy Ego in Working Toward Success. Medium. htt-ps://medium.com/illumination/why-you-should-build-a-healthy-ego-c6f473e1de57

168 Price, P. et al. Retrieved January 14, 2021. Methods of Knowing. Research Methods in Psychology 3rd Ed. Press-books. https://opentext.wsu.edu/carriecuttler/chapter/met hods-of-knowing/.

169 Belief. Oxford Languages and Google. https://languages. oup.com/googledictionary-en/

170 Leicester, J. (2008). The Nature and Purpose of Belief. *The Journal of Mind and Behavior, 29*(3), 217-237. Retrieved January 17, 2021, from http://www.jstor.org/stable/43854216

171 Popper, K. (2018, March 20). Quotation Celebration. htt-

ps://quotationcelebration.wordpress.com/2018/03/30/
the-aim-of-argument-should-not-be-victory-but-progress-
karl-popper/

172 Merriam-Webster. (n.d.). Enlightened self-interest. In *Merri-am-Webster.com dictionary*. Retrieved June 3, 2021, from https://www.merriam-webster.com/dictionary/enlightened%20self-interest

173 Joan Halifax. Read more at https://www.brainyquote.com/topics/survival

174 Thompson, T. (2016, March 15). The Illusion of Free Will. Zen Thinking.http://www.zenthinking.net/blog/the-illu-sion-of-free-will

175 Pinker, S. (2011). The Better Angels of our Nature. New York, NY: Viking.

176 Parker, K. et al. (2015, Jue11). Multiracial in America. Pew Research Center. https://www.pewsocialtrends.org/2015/06/11/multiracial-in-america/

177 "The Hard Problem of Consciousness," by Weisberg, J. The Internet Encyclopedia of *Philosophy. https://iep.utm.edu/hard-con/*, January 17, 2121.

178 Cook, G. (2020, January 14). Does Consciousness Pervade the Universe? *Scientific American* https://www.scientifi-camerican.com/article/does-consciousness-pervade-the-universe/

179 Gifter, A. (2015, April 15) The Case Against Real-ity. *The Atlantic.* https://www.theatlantic.com/science/ar-chive/2016/04/the-illusion-of-reality/479559

180 Taylor, P. (n.d.) Respect for Nature: A Theory of Environ-mental Ethics. *Princeton Universcity.* Press.https://press.princeton.edu/books/paperback/9780691150246/respect-for-nature (R.

181 https://www.robertlanzabiocentrism.com/the-grand-bio-centric-design-how-life-creates-reality/

182 Smart, J. Jamieson Carswell (2020, July 28). Materialism

Encyclopedia Britannica. https://www.britannica.com/top-ic/materialism-philosophy

183 Mayo Clinic. https://www.mayoclinic.org/healthy-life-style/consumer-health/in-depth/mindfulness-exercises/art-20046356

184 Sela, J. (2020, January 9). History of Mindfulness: From East to West and Religion to Science. *Positive Psychology.* https://positivepsychology.com/history-of-mindfulness/.

185 Ibid.

186 Troy, A.S., Shallcross, A.J., Davis, T.S. *et al.* History of Mindfulness-Based Cognitive Therapy Is Associated with Increased Cognitive Reappraisal Ability. *Mindfulness* 4, 213–222 (2013). https://doi.org/10.1007/s12671-012-0114-5 ;Tang, YI-Yuan. et al (2015, March 18). The neuroscience of mindfulness meditation. *Nature Reviews Neuroscience.* https://www.nature.com/articles/nrn3916

187 Doll, A. et al. (2016, July 1). Mindful attention to breath regulates emotions via increased amygdala–prefrontal cortex connectivity NeuroImage, Volume 134, 2016, pp. 320–327. https://www.sciencedirect.com/science/article/abs/pii/S1053811916002469

188 (n.d.) Building Resilience. *mindful.* https://www.mindful.org/meditation/mindfulness-getting-started/

189 Einstein, A. (1954). Ideas and Opinions. New York, NY. Wings Books.

Conclusion

190 Maharaj, N. (1973). I Am That. The Acorn Press

References

Abbott, A. (2015, May 26). Animal Behaviour: Inside the cunning, caring and greedy minds of fish. *Nature*. Available from: https://www.nature.com/news/animal-behaviour-inside-the-cunning-caring-and-greedy-minds-of-fish-1.17614?WT.ec_id=NATURE-20150528 (Accessed 20 March 2021)

Anderson, R. (2019, March). A Journey into the Animal Mind. *The Atlantic*. Available from: https://www.theatlantic.com/magazine/archive/2019/03/what-the-crow-knows/580726/

Asma, S. (2014, November 11). United by Feelings. *Aeon*. Available from: https://aeon.co/essays/human-culture-and-cognition-evolved-through-the-emotions

Barger, R. (2000). A Summary of Lawrence Kohlberg's Stages of Moral Development. Available from: https://www.qcc.cuny.edu/SocialSciences/ppecorino/MEDICAL_ETHICS_TEXT/Chapter_2_Ethical_Traditions/Reading-Barger-on-Kohlberg.htm (Accessed 20 March 2021)

Brakin, J. (2016. April 22). Life Will Out – What Will You Leave this World. Someday Is Now. Available from: https://somedayisnow.me/life-will-out-what-will-you-leave-this-world/

Bekoff, M. (2017, November 21) Animals Aren't Sentient and Can't Feel Pain, Tories Claim. *Psychology Today*. Available from: https://www.psychologytoday.com/us/blog/animal-emotions/201711/animals-arent-sentient-and-cant-feel-pain-tories-claim

Bellefonds, C. (2020. May 14). Why Michael Phelps Has the Perfect Body for Swimming. *Biography*. Available from: https://www.biography.com/news/michael-phelp-perfect-body-swimming

Biological Foundations of Morality. (2010, March 1819). *McFarland Center for Religion Ethics and Culture*. Available from: https://www.holycross.edu/faith-service/mcfarland-center-religion-ethics-and-culture/conferences/biological-foundations

Bloom, P. (2016) Against Empathy. Harper Collins. New York.

p.94.

Blumenfeld, R. (2020, March 21). How a 15,000-Year-Old Human Bone Could Help You through the Coronacrisis. *Forbes*. Available from: https://www.forbes.com/sites/remyblumenfeld/2020/03/21/how-a-15000-year-old-human-bone-could-help-you-through-the--coronavirus/#d32569637e9b

Bourg Carter, S. (2012, January 31). 6 Reasons You Should Spend More Time Alone. *Psychology Today*. Available from: https://www.psychologytoday.com/us/blog/high-octane-women/201201/6-reasons-you-should-spend-more-time-alone

Briet, C. (2018, August 27). How to know it's Time to Let Go of Someone You Love. *Time*. Available from: https://time.com/5373451/break-up-someone-love/

Britannica, T. Editors of Encyclopaedia (2020, January 31). Determinism. Encyclopedia Britannica. https://www.britannica.com/topic/determinism

Browning, C. (1998). Ordinary Men. Harper Perennial. New York.

Bruss, J. (2018, October 31). Quora. Available from: https://www.quora.com/Are-humans-manipulative-by-nature

Belief. Oxford Languages and Google. Available from: https://languages.oup.com/google dictionary-en/

Cahill, L. (2012. October 1). His Brain Her Brain. *Scientific American*. Available from: https://www.scientificamerican.com/article/his-brain-her-brain-2012-10-23/

Cherry, K. (2020. June 29). Overview of the 6 Major Theories of Emotion. *Verywell Mind*. https://www.verywellmind.com/theories-of-emotion-2795717

Cherry, K. (2020, June 25). The Origins of Psychology. Very Well Mind. Available from: https://www.verywellmind.com/a-brief-history-of-psychology-through-the-years-2795245

Cherry, K. (2019, September 28). Freud's Id, Ego, and Superego. Very Well Mind. Available from: https://www.verywellmind.com/the-id-ego-and-superego-2795951

Cherry, K. Freud's. Id.

Cherry, K. (2020, June 3). Flow Can Help You Achieve Goals. *Verywellmind.* Available from: https://www.verywellmind.com/ what-is-flow-2794768

Clabough, E. (2016, March 4). Survival of the Most Empathetic. Psychology Today. Available from: https://www. psychologytoday.com/us/blog/neuroparent/201603/survival-the-most-empathetic

CNRS. (2016, April 27). A single-celled organism capable of learning. *ScienceDaily.* Available from: www.sciencedaily.com/ releases/2016/04/160427081533.htm

Conversation. (March 17, 2021). Selfish or Selfless. *Neuroscience News.* Available from: https://neurosciencenews.com/ human-nature-selfish-selfless-18057/?fbclid=IwAR3gZk4ke-CHnEQza6BJ8QfFTGjOWE_UcsceHqXF78k_ fyO79S7AQViuMu4

Cook-Greuter, S. (2013, December) Nine Levels of Increasing Embrace in Ego Development: a Full-Spectrum Theory Of Vertical Growth And Meaning Making. *Goodreads.* Available from: http://www.cook-greuter.com/Cook-Greuter%209%20 levels%20paper%20new%201.1%2714%2097p%5B1%5D.pdft

Cook, G. (2020, January 14). Does Consciousness Pervade the Universe? *Scientific American.* Available from: https://www. scientificamerican.com/article/does-consciousness-pervade-the-universe/

Cross-Eyed Pianist. (2020, May 25). A state of ecstasy: flow. *The Cross-Eyed Pianist.* Available from: https://crosseyedpianist. com/2020/05/25/a-state-of-ecstasy-flow/.

Csikszentmihalyi, M. (2004, February) *Flow, the secret to happiness.* [Video file] Available from: https://www.ted.com/talks/ mihaly_csikszentmihalyi_flow_the_secret_to_happiness/ transcript?language=en

Darwin, C.R. (1871) The Descent of Man. Penguin. New York, N.Y.

Dash, M. (2011, December 23). The Story of the WWI Christmas

Truce. Smithsonian Magazine. Available from: https: //www. smithsonianmag.com/history/the-story-of-the-wwi-christmas-truce-11972213/

Depersonalization-derealization disorder. (n.d.) *Mayo Clinic.* Available from: https://www.mayoclinic.org/diseases-cond itions/depersonalization-derealization-disorder/symptoms-causes/syc-20352911

DeWall, Franz. (2005, September 1). The Evolution of Empathy. *Greater Good Magazine.* Available from: *https://greatergood. berkeley.edu/article/item/the_evolution_of_empathy*

Dingman, M. (2014. May 17). Know Your Brain: Prefrontal cortex. Neuroscientific ally Challenged. Available from: https: https:// www.neuroscientificallychallenged.com/blog/2014/5/16/know-your-brain-prefrontal-cortex

Dolan, E. (2019, August 23). Ingroup – versus – outgroup thinking warps the moral principles of liberals and conservatives. Available from: https: PsyPost.https://www.psypost. org/2019/08/ingroup-versus-outgroup-thinking-warps-the-moral-principles-of-liberals-and-conservatives-54277

Doll, A. et al. (2016, July 1). Mindful attention to breath regulates emotions via increased amygdala–prefrontal cortex connectivity NeuroImage, Volume 134, 2016, pp. 320–327. https://www. sciencedirect.com/science/article/abs/pii/S1053811916002469

Education.com. (2014, May 14). Lucky Age 7: why and How kids Change. *Education.com.* Available from: https: https://www. education.com/magazine/article/Lucky_7._

Einstein, A. (1954). Ideas and Opinions. New York, NY. Wings Books.

Fromm, E. (1964) The Heart of Man. Harper and Row. New York p. 80, 86.

Gagliano, M. (2021). Plant Behaviour & Cognition. Scientific Research. Available from: https://www.monicagagliano.com

George, J. (2006. February 17). Polar bear no match for fearsome mother in Ivujivik. *Numatsiaq News.* Available from: https:

https://science.howstuffworks.com/life/inside-the-mind/
human-brain/how-stress-works.htm

Gholipour, B. (2019, September 10). A Famous Argument Against Free Will. *The Atlantic*. Available from: https:https://www.theatlantic.com/health/archive/2019/09/free-will-bereitschaftspotential/597736/

Gholipour, B. (2019, March 21). Philosophers and neuroscientists join forces to see whether science can solve the mystery of free will. Science Magazine. Available from: https:https://www.sciencemag.org/news/2019/03/philosophers-and-neuroscientists-join-forces-see-whether-science-can-solve-mystery-free?utm_campaign=SciMag&utm_source=JHubbard&utm_medium=Facebook

Gifter, A. (2015, April 15)The Case Against Reality. *The Atlantic*. Available from: https:https://www.theatlantic.com/science/archive/2016/04/the-illusion-of-reality/479559/

Gildenhuys, P. (2019). "Natural Selection", *The Stanford Encyclopedia of Philosophy* (Winter 2019 Edition), Edward N. Zalta (ed.), URL = Available from: <https://plato.stanford.edu/archives/win2019/entries/natural-selection/>.

Goldhill, O. (2015, September 20). Neuroscience backs up the Buddhist belief that "the self" isn't constant but ever-changing. Quartz. Available from: https: https://qz.com/506229/neuroscience-backs-up-the-buddhist-belief-that-the-self-isnt-constant-but-ever-changing/.

Gopnik, A. (2020, July 23). Learning without a brain *Wall Street Journal*. Available from: https:https://www.wsj.com/articles/learning-without-a-brain-11595527115

Haidt, J. (2006). The Happiness Hypothesis: finding Modern truth in ancient wisdom. New York, Basic Books pp. 4–5

Haidt, J. (2013). The Righteous Mind: Why Good People Are Divided by Politics and Religion. New York. Vintage Books. pp. 71–86.

Haidt, J. (2008). Morality. *Perspectives On Psychological Science.*

https://people.stern.nyu.edu/jhaidt/articles/haidt.2008.morality.
pub052.pdf

Hari, J. (2018, January 20). Lost Connections, *Bloomsbury* USA. p.77

Harnad, S. (2016). Animal Sentence: The other-minds problem. *Animal Sentience* Vol. 1 (1). Available from: https: // animalstudiesrepository.org/animsent/

Harris, S. (2012). Free Will. New York, NY. Free Press. p. 9

Harari Y. (2020 September 13). Why Fascism is so tempting. Ted Ed. YouTube. https://ed.ted.com/lessons/why-fascism-is-so-tempting-and-how-your-data-could-power-it-yuval-noah-ha rari?fbclid=IwAR3JSJaGsxAfpP4hUjdUmhWjKQkJyejrFh2H-itQlIBKi40loQ0UCt4GUu0

Hawking, S and Mlodinow, L. (2010, October 1). The Elusive Theory of Everything. Scientific American. Available from: https://www.scientificamerican.com/article/the-elusive-thoery-of-everything/

Hero's Journey: Definition and Step-by-Step Guide. (2021, April 28). *Reedsyblog*. Available from: https://blog.reedsy.com/guide/story-structure/heros-journey/

Holt, J. (2011, November 25). Two Brans Running. *New York Times*. Available from: https://www.nytimes.com/2011/11/27/books/review/thinking-fast-and-slow-by-daniel-kahneman-book-review.html

Hoff, M. (2020, November 12). Information Gained, Stored, and Transferred Without Brains. *Ask Nature*. https://asknature.org/strategy/brainless-slime-molds-both-learn-and-teach/

Halifax, J. Read more at https://www.brainyquote.com/topics/survival

Hogenboom, M. (2016, August 23). Why bullying is such a successful evolutionary strategy. *Earth*. Available from: http://www.bbc.com/earthstory20160822-why-bullying-is-such-a-successful-evolutionary-strategy

Herndon, E. (2018, February 6). What are multiple intelligences and how do they affect learning? [Web log post]. Available from: https://www.cornerstone.edu/blogs/lifelong-learning-matters/post/what-are-multiple-intelligences-and-how-do-they-affect-learning

Itzhak, F. et. al. (2020, June). Internally Generated Preactivation of Single Neurons in Human Medial Frontal Cortex Predicts Volition p.548. Cell Press. Available from: http://braininstprd. wpengine.com/wp-content/uploads/2020/06/gk2630.pdf.

Johns Hopkins University. (2020, June 8). Philosophy lab. Test' finds objective vision impossible. Medical Press. Available from: https://medicalxpress.com/news/2020-06-philosophy-lab-vision-impossible.html.

Jung, C.G. (1966). *Collected Works*, Princeton University Press vol. 6, paragraph 643.

Jung C. G. (1966 "Introduction," *Collected Works,* Princeton University Press vol. 12, paragraph 44.

Kahn, N., and Shen, J. (2020, February 20). Brian Greene talks about the Physics of Free Will at the Science Center Lecture. The Harvard Crimson. Available from: J.https://www.thecrimson. com/article/2020/2/20/brian-greene-physics-will/.

Keeton, CP, et al. (2008, April 22). Sense of Control Predicts Depressive and Anxious Symptoms Across the Transition to Parenthood. PMC. Available from: https://www.ncbi.nlm.nih. gov/pmc/articles/PMC2834184/

Kaufman, C. (2012, August 12). Why Bad Guys Think They're Good Guys. *Psychology Today.* Available from: https://www. psychologytoday.com/us/blog/psychology-writers/201208/ why-bad-guys-think-theyre-good-guys

Klien, E. (2017, February 28). Yuval Harari, author of Sapiens, on how meditation made him a better historian. Available from: https://www.vox.com/2017/2/28/14745596/yuval-harari-sapiens-interview-meditation-ezra-klein

Koch, C. (2018 June 1). What Is Consciousness. *Scientific American.* Available from: https://www.scientificamerican.com/article/ what-is-consciousness/

Kolbert, E. (2017, February 20). Why Facts Don't Change Our Minds. New Yorker. Available from: https://www.newyorker.com/magazine/2017/02/27/why-facts-dont-change-our-minds?fbclid=IwAR3FDr_OsE22OFivtjTnaBl6pl37x14oSnBANtGlVShLa8uj8Kl3pyFmCi8

Konnikova, M. (2015, June 12.) The Real Lesson of the Stanford Prison Experiment. The New Yorker. Available from: https://www.newyorker.com/science/maria-konnikova/the-real-lesson-of-the-stanford-prison-experiment.

Kotler, Steven. (n.d.) Frequently Asked Questions on Flow. Available from: https://www.stevenkotler.com/rabbit-hole/frequently-asked-questions-on-flo

Cherry, K. (2020, June 3). Flow Can Help You Achieve Goals. *Verywellmind.* https://www.verywellmind.com/what-is-flow-27 94768

Klien, E. (2017, February 28). Yuval Harari, author of Sapiens, on how meditation made him a better historian. Available from: https://www.vox.com/2017/2/28/14745596/yuval-harari-sapiens-interview-meditation-ezra-klein

Lanza, R. Biocentrism (n.d.) Available from: https://www.robertlanzabiocentrism.com/the-grand-biocentric-design-how-life-creates-reality/

Leicester, J. (2008). The Nature and Purpose of Belief. *The Journal of Mind and Behavior, 29*(3), 217–237. Retrieved January 17, 2021. Available from: http://www.jstor.org/stable/43854216

Lawrence Kohlberg. Blog Last Update: 07-06-2015. Available from: https://www.goodtherapy.org/famous-psychologists/lawrence-kohlberg.html

Levin, M. (2020, October,13). Cognition all the way down. *Aeon.* Available from: https://aeon.co/essays/how-to-understand-cells-tissues-and-organisms-as-agents-with-agendas?utm_source=Aeon+Newsletter&utm_campaign=c3aa091573-EMAIL_CAMPAIGN_2020_10_16_01_06&utm_medium=email&utm_term=0_411a82e59d-c3aa091573-70902379

Loevinger, J. (2020, January 31). The Stages of Ego Development Theory according to Jane Loevinger. *American Institute for Learning and Human Development*. Available from: https://www.institute4learning.com/2020/01/31/the-stages-of-ego-development-according-to-jane-loevinger/.

Kolbert, E. (2017, February 20). Why Facts Don't Change Our Minds. New Yorker. Available from: https://www.newyorker.com/magazine/2017/02/27/why-facts-dont-change-ourminds?fbclid=IwAR3FDr_OsE22OFivtjTnaBl6pl37x14oSnBANtGlVShLa8uj8Kl3pyFmCi8

Lucas, M. (2010, June 30). Why Independence Isn't Worth The Fireworks. *Psychology Today*. Available from: https://www.psychologytoday.com/us/blog/rewire-your-brain-love/201006/why-independence-isnt-worth-the-fireworks

Magazine. https://greatergood.berkeley.edu/article/item/the_evolution_of_empathy

Maharaj, N. (1973). I Am That. The Acorn Press. Durham, N.C.

Maslow, A. (2013). A Theory of Human Motivation. *Martino Publishing*. Mansfield Centre CT.

Mayo Clinic. Available from: https://www.mayoclinic.org/healthy-lifestyle/consumer-health/in-depth/mindfulness-exercises/art-20046356

McLeod, S. (2020, December 29). Maslow's Hierarchy of Needs. *Simply Psychology*. Available from: https://www.simplypsychology.org/maslow.html

Merkur, D. (2010, January) Erich Fromm' Humanistic Psychoanalysist. *Brill*. Available from: https://brill.com/view/book/9789042028609/B9789042028609-s005.xml

Merriam-Webster. (n.d.). Enlightened self-interest. In *Merriam-Webster.com dictionary*. Available from: https://www.merriam-webster.com/dictionary/enlightened%20self-interest

Morell, V (2017. February 13). Monkeys master a key sign of self-awareness: recognizing their reflections. *Science*. Available from: https://www.sciencemag.org/news/2017/02/monkeys-master-key-sign-self-awareness-recognizing-their-reflections

Merriam-Webster. (n.d.). Ego. In Merriam-Webster.com dictionary. Available from: 2020, from https://www.merriam-webster.com/dictionary/ego.

Milton, J. (2000). Paradise Lost. New York, NY: Penguin Books.

Mindful. (n.d.) Getting Started with Mindfulness. *Mindful.* Available from: https://www.mindful.org/meditation/mindfulness-getting-started/

Mohammed, H. (2020, February 28). Why do girls mature faster than boys? *Baron News.* Available from: https://www.baronnews.com/2020/02/28/why-do-girls-mature-faster-than-boys/

Merenus, M. (2020, June 9). Gardner's Theory of Multiple Intelligences. *Simply Psychology.* Available from: https://www.simplypsychology.org/multiple-intelligences.html

(Merriam-Webster. (n.d.). Fatalism. In Merriam-Webster.com dictionary. Available from: from https://www.merriam-webster.com/dictionary/fatalism.

Nowak, M. and Roch, S. (2007, March 7). Upstream reciprocity and the evolution of gratitude. *National Center Biotechnological Information.* Available from: https://www.ncbi.nlm.nih.gov/pmc/articles/PMC2197219/

Oakley D. Halligan, P. (2017, November 14). Chasing the Rainbow: The Non-conscious Nature of Being. Frontiers in Psychology. Available from: https://www.frontiersin.org/articles/10.3389/fpsyg.2017.01924/full

Oakley D. Halligan, P. (2017, November 17) What if consciousness is not what drives the human mind. The Conversation. Available from: https://theconversation.com/what-if-consciousness-is-not-what-drives-the-human-mind-86785.

Origins of Virtue - Summary" eNotes Publishing Ed. eNotes Editorial. eNotes.com, Inc.eNotes.com Origins of Virtue – Summary" eNotes Publishing Ed. eNotes Editorial. eNotes.com. Available from: https://www.enotes.com/topics/origins-virtue

Parker, K. et al. (2015, Jue11). Multiracial in America. Pew Research Center. Available from: https://www.pewsocialtrends. org/2015/06/11/multiracial-in-america/

Pederson, D. (2020, August 18). Perception, Medium. Available from: https://medium.com/personal-growth/perception-ca058 251e197

Penn State. (2019, February 25). Some personal beliefs and morals may stem from genetics. *Science News*. Available from: https:// www.sciencedaily.com/releases/2019/02/190225145632.htm

Pinker, S. (2011). The Better Angels of our Nature. New York, NY: Viking.

Platts-Mills, B. (2020, October 20). Memory involves the whole body. Psyche. Available from: https://psyche.co/ideas/memory-involves-the-whole-body-its-how-the-self-defies-amnesia? fbclid=IwAR1YzGcDvLC6ASSQFkt6I_mEAzfsa2zg9NcQ_ BLHnRDikNRQmB2Vlyx4a5c

Popper, K. (2018, March 20). Quotation Celebration. Available from:https://quotationcelebration.wordpress.com/2018/03/30/ the-aim-of-argument-should-not-be-victory-but-progress-karl-popper/

Price, P. et al. Methods of Knowing. Research Methods in Psychology 3ʳᵈ Ed. Pressbooks. Available from: https://opentext. wsu.edu/carriecuttler/chapter/methods-of-knowing/.

Priebe, H. (2015, May 13). Be the Anti-Hero of Your Own Life. Thought Catalog. Available from: https://thoughtcatalog.com/ heidi-priebe/2015/05/be-the-anti-hero-of-your-own-life/

Rayner, T. (2008, April 7). Heraclitus, change and flow. *Philosophy for Change*. Available from: https://philosophyforchange. wordpress.com/2008/04/07/heraclitus-on-change/

Rey, G. (2020, August 8). Philosophy of Mind. Encyclopedia Britannica. Available from: https://www.britannica.com/topic/ philosophy-of-mind

Reynolds, E. (2020, October 20). After Cheating on a Test, People

Claim to Have Known the Answers Anyway. Research Digest. Available from: https://digest.bps.org.uk/2020/10/20/after-cheating-on-a-test-people-claim-to-have-known-the-answers-anyway/?fbclid=IwAR0bVvQIjJh4j1k1c3Y_9w1mEqNuXkZPS Gm9LSc_tXxTXirX328EXZCGTQM.

Resnick, B. (2018, June 6). The "marshmallow test" said patience was a key to success. A new replication tells us s'more. Vox. Available from: https://www.vox.com/science-and-health/2018/6/6/17413000/marshmallow-test-replication-mischel-psychology.

Rice, C. (2015, June 24). A Nation that still falls short of its ideals. *The Baltimore Sun*. Available from: https://www.baltimoresun.com/opinion/readers-respond/bs-ed-racism-letter-20150624-story.html

Rodriquez, E. (2018, Nov. 16). Ego. The Encyclopedia Britannica. Available from:https://www.britannica.com/topic/ego-philosophy-and-psychology.

Rossine, et al. (2020, March 19). Eco-evolutionary significance of "loners." *Plos Biology*. Available from: https://journals.plos.org/plosbiology/article?id=10.1371%2Fjournal.pbio.3000642&fbclid=IwAR0QTM3osZJiJY9_9IUzDlfSV8xHf5kkAI6d1aG33PODN-IuiblnfS1tyTE

Sachs, S. (1998, August 16). Age of Reason; A chilling Crime and a Question: What's in a child's mind? *The New York Times*. Available from: https://www.nytimes.com/1998/08/16/weekinreview/the-age-of-reason-a-chilling-crime-and-a-question-what-s-in-a-child-s-mind.html

Samayoa, W. (2020, Nov. 20). Why You Should Build a Healthy Ego in Working Toward Success. Medium. Available from: https://medium.com/illumination/why-you-should-build-a-healthy-ego-c6f473e1de57

Sapolsky, R. (2017). Behave: The Biology of Humans at Our Best and Worst. New York, NY. Penguin.

Sapolsky, R. (2006, April 6). The 2% Difference. *Discover Mag.*

Available from:https://www.discovermagazine.com/planet-earth/the-2-difference

Schultz, N. (2007. June 25). Altruistic chimps act for the benefit of others. *New Scientist*. Available from: https://www.newscientist.com/article/dn12132-altruistic-chimps-act-for-the-benefit-of-others/

Shaeffer, l. (2020, August 23) The most successful strategy in life. The Pennsylvania Capitol Star. Available from: https://www.penncapital-star.com/commentary/the-most-successful-strategy-in-life-lloyd-e-sheaffer/

Schmidt, M. (2020. March 13). Why Coronavirus Is Turning People into Hoarders: A Q&A on the Psychology of Pandemics *Discover*. Available from: https://www.discovermagazine.com/health/why-coronavirus-is-turning-people-into-hoarders-a-q-and-a-on-the-psychology

Schoenherr, N. (2020, March 6). Book explores "rugged individualism" and its impact on inequality in America *The Source*. Available from: https://source.wustl.edu/2020/03/book-explores-rugged-individualism-and-its-impact-on-inequality-in-america/

Sela, J. (2020, January 9). History of Mindfulness: From East to West and Religion to Science. *Positive Psychology*. Available from: https://positivepsychology.com/history-of-mindfulness/.

Shaun, N. (2008, August 19). Free Will versus the Programmed Brain. Scientific American. Available from: https://www.scientificamerican.com/article/free-will-vs-programmed-brain/

Smart, J. Jamieson Carswell (2020, July 28). Materialism. Encyclopedia Britannica. Available from: https://www.britannica.com/topic/materialism-philosophy

Smith, E. (2015, December 2). Is Human Morality a Product of Evolution. *The Atlantic*. Available from: https://www.theatlantic.com/health/archive/2015/12/evolution-of-morality-social-humans-and-apes/418371/

Solondz, Todd. Available from:

Read more at https://www.brainyquote.com/topics/survival

Soon, C.S. et al. (2008, June). Unconscious determinants of free decisions in the human brain. Research Gate. Available from: https://www.researchgate.net/publication/5443390_Unco nscious_determinants_of_free_decisions_in_the_human_ brain.

Stanford Encyclopedia of Philosophy. (2006 April 26). Compatibilism. Available from: https://plato.stanford.edu/ entries/compatibilism/.

Steimer, T. (2002. September 4). The biology of-fear-and anxiety. *National Library of Medicine.* Available from: https://pubmed. ncbi.nlm.nih.gov/22033741/#affiliation-1

Stierwalt, R. (2020, April 4) How Can You Tell if You Have Perfect Pitch. *Scientific American.* Available from: https://www. scientificamerican.com/article/how-can-you-tell-if-you-have-perfect-pitch/

Suchman, N. PhD et al. Ego Development Psychopathology, and Parenting Problems in Substance-Abusing Mothers. *National Center for Biotechnology Information.* Available from: https:// www.ncbi.nlm.nih.gov/pmc/articles/PMC2729054/

Suarez, S. Pacey, A (2005. November 04). Sperm transport in the female reproductive tract. *Human Reproduction Update.* https:// academic.oup.com/humupd/article/12/1/23/607817

Survival. (n.d.). In Merriam-webster.com dictionary. Available from: https://www.merriam-webster.com/dictionary/survival

Tang, YI-Yuan. et al (2015, March 18). The neuroscience of mindfulness meditation. *Nature Reviews Neuroscience.* Available from: https://www.nature.com/articles/nrn3916

Tartakovsky, M. (2018, July 8). Owning Our dark Sides. Psych Central. Available from: https://psychcentral.com/blog/owning-our-dark-sides/.

Taylor, P. (n.d.) Respect for Nature: A Theory of Environmental Ethics. *Princeton University Press.* Available from: https://press. princeton.edu/books/paperback/9780691150246/respect-for-nature (*R*.

Thompson, T. (2016, March 15). The Illusion of Free Will. Zen Thinking. Available from: http://www.zenthinking.net/blog/the-illusion-of-free-will

Travis, C and Aronson, E. (2007). Mistakes Were Made (but not by me) Boston, Mariner Books. New York, N.Y. pp. 15–18

Troy, A.S., Shallcross, A.J., Davis, T.S. *et al.* History of Mindfulness-Based Cognitive Therapy Is Associated with Increased Cognitive Reappraisal Ability. *Mindfulness* 4, 213–222 (2013). Available from: https://doi.org/10.1007/s12671-012-0114-5

Vaupel. J. (2018. January 23). Women live longer than men even during severe famines and epidemics. *PNAS*. Available from: https://www.pnas.org/content/115/4/E832

Wadi'h, H. (2004. December 10). When does 2+2 not equal 4? People's World. Available from: https://www.peoplesworld.org/article/when-does-2-2-not-equal-4/.

Weisberg, J. (2121. January 17). The Hard Problem of Consciousness, *The Internet Encyclopedia of Philosophy*. Available from: https://iep.utm.edu/hard-con/,

Williams, R. (2019. December 5). Single-Celled Organism Appears to Make Decisions. *The Scientist*. Available from: https://www.the-scientist.com/news-opinion/single-celled-organism-appears-to-make decisions-66818

Woodruff, M. (2020. July 3). Do fish have faces. *Aeon*. Available from: https://aeon.co/essays/fish-are-nothing-like-us-except-that-they-are-sentient-being

Woolley, D, and Ghossainy, M. (2013, September) revisiting the Fantasy-Reality Distinction: Children as Naïve Skeptics. PMC. Available from: https://www.ncbi.nlm.nih.gov/pmc/articles/PMC3689871/

Xinhua. (2019, September 16). Unicellular organisms can learn, remember: Israeli-Spanish research *XINHUANET*. Available from: http://www.xinhuanet.com/english/2019-09/16/c_138393828.htm

About the Author

Jerry Pannone attended San Francisco State University, where he received his teaching credential and Master's degree in Music. During this period he also attended the Ali Akbar Khan College of North Indian Music. Although his main area of emphasis has been in teaching, he has also composed two ballets, two choral ensemble works, and several works for jazz band and chamber ensembles.

He has taught grades ranging from elementary through high school in San Mateo, Oakland, and San Francisco, California, while continuing to pursue his professional performing career. Mr. Pannone has been a conductor for the San Francisco School District Honor Orchestra, and for the past 30 years taught humanities, critical thinking, and music at the San Francisco School of the Arts High School (now renamed the Ruth Asawa School of the Arts). He also founded a program on ethics, which was part of the National High School Ethics Bowl (NHSEB) and partnered graduate students from the San Francisco State University Philosophy Department with students from two San Francisco high schools.

Mr. Pannone has received numerous awards for teaching, including the San Francisco Symphony's 2003 Agnes Albert Award for excellence in music education and the 2009 Teacher of the Year Award for California State Senate District 8. He received the California Music Educators Association's Bay Area Life Time Achievement Award in 2018 for exemplary service and contributions to the music education profession.

Mr. Pannone has also had a life-long interest in philosophy and psychology, as well as a deep, abiding love of metaphysics, all of which have contributed to the subject of this book.

PSYCHE BOOKS

PSYCHE BOOKS
PSYCHOLOGY

Psyche Books cover all aspects of psychology and matters relating to the head.

The study of the mind - interactions, behaviors, functions; developing and expanding our understanding of self.

Psychology: All forms, all disciplines including business, criminal, educational, sport. Therapies: clinical analysis, CBT, counselling, hypnosis, NLP, psychoanalysis, psychodrama, psychotherapy, role-play.

Archetypes, behavioral science, CAM therapies, experimental work, popular psychology, psychological studies, neuroscience. Including but not restricted to: Behavior, brain games, personality, mental health, mind coaching, nature of the mind, treatment strategies, unconscious mind.

If you have enjoyed this book, why not tell other readers by posting a review on your preferred book site.

Recent bestsellers from PSYCHE BOOKS are:

The Chi of Change
How Hypnotherapy Can Help You Heal and Turn Your Life
Around - Regardless of Your Past
Peter Field
A ground breaking book that will change forever the way you
think about your feelings and emotions!
Paperback: 978-1-78279-351-9 ebook: 978-1-78279-350-2

Emotional Life
Managing Your Feelings to Make the Most of Your Precious Time
on Earth How to Gain Mastery Over Your Feelings
Doreen Davy
Emotional Life explains how we can harness our own emotional
power in order to live happier, healthier and more fulfilling lives.
Paperback: 978-1-78279-276-5 ebook: 978-1-78279-275-8

Creating Trance and Hypnosis Scripts
Gemma Bailey
A well-known hypnotherapist reveals her secret tips on how to
help others quit smoking, lose weight and beat the blues.
Paperback: 978-1-84694-197-9

Depression: Understanding the Black Dog
Stephanie June Sorrell
This accessible work addresses a universal health issue with a
toolbag yielding the ways depression manifests and insight into
the treatments available.
Paperback: 978-1-78279-165-2 ebook: 978-1-78279-174-4

Smashing Depression
Escaping the Prison and Finding a Life
Terence Watts
Depression is an insidious enemy, gradually eroding confidence and willpower... but this book restores the spirit and strength to fight back - and win!
Paperback: 978-1-78279-619-0 ebook: 978-1-78279-618-3

Why Men Like Straight Lines and Women Like Polka Dots
Gender and Visual Psychology
Gloria Moss
Discover how men and women perceive the world differently and why they won't agree on the colour or shape of the sofa!
Paperback: 978-1-84694-857-2 ebook: 978-1-84694-708-7

Head versus Heart
Michael Hampson
The most important new material on the enneagram in thirty years, Head Versus Heart questions how we engage with the world around us.
Paperback: 978-1-90381-692-9

Mastering Your Self, Mastering Your World
Living by the Serenity Prayer
John William Reich
Mastery over the events of our life is key to our well-being; this book explains how to achieve that mastery.
Paperback: 978-1-78279-727-2 ebook: 978-1-78279-726-5

The Secret Life of Love and Sex
Making Relationships Work and What to Do If They Don't
Terence Watts
Men and women think differently and 'work' differently - but they don't know that! SO sometimes a white lie or a secret is a good thing...
Paperback: 978-1-78279-464-6 ebook: 978-1-78279-463-9

Powerful Mind Through Self-Hypnosis
A Practical Guide to Complete Self-Mastery
Cathal O'Briain
Powerful Mind Through Self-Hypnosis is the definitive book, teaching self-hypnosis as a pure and natural form of self-healing.
Paperback: 978-1-84694-298-3 ebook: 978-1-78099-761-2

Readers of ebooks can buy or view any of these bestsellers by clicking on the live link in the title. Most titles are published in paperback and as an ebook. Paperbacks are available in traditional bookshops. Both print and ebook formats are available online.

Find more titles and sign up to our readers' newsletter at http://www.johnhuntpublishing.com/mind-body-spirit. Follow us on Facebook at https://www.facebook.com/OBooks and Twitter at https://twitter.com/obooks.